The Last Eleven Days
of
Earl Durand

ALSO BY JERRED METZ

Speak Like Rain, poetry

The Temperate Voluptuary, poetry

Angels in the House, poetry

Drinking the Dipper Dry: Nine Plain-Spoken Lives, prose

Three Legs Up, Cold as Stone: Six Legs Down, Blood and Bone, poetry

Halley's Comet, 1910: Fire in the Sky, prose

The Last Eleven Days
~ *of* ~
Earl Durand

JERRED METZ

HIGH PLAINS PRESS

FIRST PRINTING

10 9 8 7 6 5 4 3 2 1

Library of Congress Cataloging-in-Publication Data

Metz, Jerred
The last eleven days of Earl Durand / Jerred Metz.
p. cm.
Includes bibliographical references and index.
ISBN 0-931271-72-X (hardcover)
ISBN 0-931271-73-8 (trade paper)
1. Durand, Earl, 1913-1939.
2. Brigands and robbers--Wyoming--Powell--Biography.
3. Poachers--Wyoming--Powell--Biography.
4. Bank robberies--Wyoming--Powell--History.
I. Title.
HV6653.D8M48   2004
364.1'092--dc22
2004010151

HIGH PLAINS PRESS
539 CASSA ROAD
GLENDO, WYOMING 82213

CATALOG AVAILABLE
WWW.HIGHPLAINSPRESS.COM

For Sarah, Zachary, and Ravenna

Durand Likely to Become Wild West Legend

No matter what new cruelties and depredations may be perpetuated by Durand before he meets his inevitable fate, those stories will endure through future generations and will become a part of the saga of the west—the west that even in the twentieth century produced a man who knew no law but his own.

Cody Enterprise

ↅ ↅ ↅ ↅ ↅ ↅ

If the case of that Wyoming bandit were not a grim business involving four slayings, we would be tempted to say that it is another instance of nature imitating art. There has been such an outburst of outlawry on the screen and stage that it was only a question of time before the Western desperado would come to life in the news.

New York Times

ↅ ↅ ↅ ↅ ↅ ↅ

Powell, Wyo., March 25 [1939]—(A.P.)—To the saga of the wild west will be added tales of the strange, lonely life of a 26-year-old mountain Tarzan who came back to civilization for a spectacular, bizarre exit.

Earl Durand, game poacher and slayer who was killed Friday while robbing a Powell bank after he had eluded capture for nine days in his mountain hideouts, is destined to become a topic of folklore.

The most imaginative creator of pulp melodrama never, in his wildest dreams, produced as wild a story as Durand lived in his last ten days. If it had been portrayed on the screen, no one would have believed it could be real.

Denver Post

CONTENTS

CHRONOLOGY

THE LAST ELEVEN DAYS OF EARL DURAND: MARCH 13-24, 1939

Monday, March 13: A hunting party is caught poaching elk west of Cody. Earl Durand, the instigator, slips away, but the other three are arrested: farmer Emil Knopp, his son Ronnie, and a neighbor boy. Durand spends the night on Rattlesnake Mountain. The judge sentences Emil Knopp to sixty days in the Cody jail and releases the two boys.

Tuesday, March 14: Before sunrise Durand kills a local rancher's calf, then makes his way back to Rattlesnake Mountain. Sheriff Frank Blackburn is out of town, but an informal posse finds, captures, and arrests Durand. The judge fines Earl and sentences him to sixty days in the Cody jail.

Thursday, March 16: Earl breaks jail, first injuring deputy sheriff Noah Riley, then forcing the deputy to drive him to the Durand farmstead near Powell. When law officers Chuck Lewis and D.M. Baker arrive there, Earl shoots and kills them. After neighbor Virginia Turner arrives, Durand flees. He visits the Glasgow home nearby, taking a rifle, while Riley limps to the neighboring Smith farm to warn them. Cody lawyer Milward Simpson learns of the jailbreak and, in the sheriff's absence, organizes a posse to track the killer.

Thursday, March 16 through Monday, March 20: Durand's whereabouts are not known. Sheriff Frank Blackburn returns to Cody and leads the posse, without success. Ed McNeely, Vern Spencer, Mel Stonehouse, and Bill Garlow are among the possemen.

Tuesday, March 21: Durand appears at the farmhouses of several neighbors, gathering supplies. At the Smith farm, young Dick gives the outlaw a haircut and watches him shave off his beard. Possemen pursue Durand from farm to farm, glimpsing him fleetingly, but he eludes them.

Wednesday, March 22: Before sunrise Durand forces an elderly farm couple to drive him to Beartooth Mountain. The man reports the incident, and Sheriff Blackburn gathers the posse at the foot of the mountain, establishing headquarters at a ranch cabin. Harry Moore is his radio operator. One group of possemen locates the renegade in an inaccessible spot. Two undeputized tagalongs rush the hideout, but Durand's bullets kill them. (Durand takes a stolen deputy sheriff's badge from one of his victims; it will come in handy two days later.) At nightfall the sheriff calls in the posse and arranges for Montana National Guardsmen to join them the next morning. He also directs a local pilot, Bill Monday, to equip his plane with tear gas and dynamite bombs.

Thursday, March 23: Preparations to flush out the killer continue. Durand is believed to be still somewhere on the mountain, possibly headed over a pass to Clarks Fork. The sheriff and a dozen possemen retrieve the bodies of the two dead men on the mountain. The National Guardsmen are in camp when the posse returns.

Friday, March 24: Bill Monday's early flight reveals that Durand has disappeared from his hideout. Meanwhile Durand leaves the mountain and, impersonating a deputy, catches a ride with radio operator Moore and two passengers. Hijacking the car, Durand visits his parents, then ditches his hostages and drives to Powell. There he robs the First National Bank; among those terrorized are customer Vastalee Dutton, cashier Maurice Knutson, and bank president R. A. Nelson. When Durand pushes three of his victims out the door, one of them, John Gawthrop, is slain by a bystander. From across the street, seventeen-year-old Tip Cox shoots Durand, who then finishes the job with a shot to his own neck. Bill Monday relays word of Durand's death to Blackburn — still on Beartooth Mountain — while coroner and undertaker Ray Easton prepares the body of the West's last outlaw for burial.

INTRODUCTION

IN THE EARLY 1930s newspapers and magazines followed the crimes, exploits, and misdeeds of Bonnie and Clyde, "Pretty Boy" Floyd, "Baby Face" Nelson, and John Dillinger. These desperadoes and criminals lived a two-year-long spree of bank robberies, kidnappings, and killings, eluding capture and arrest and even escaping from jail. Bonnie and Clyde prowled Oklahoma and Texas. Dillinger and his gang robbed banks in Indiana, Illinois, Wisconsin, Ohio, and Iowa —ten heists in a little less than a year. After robbing forty banks and committing ten murders, Charles Floyd was killed by an FBI agent. Nelson was a heartless criminal from adolescence on—car thief, bootlegger, bank robber. By the time he was shot down, he had killed several men, including three FBI agents.

These men and molls gone bad were really only smalltime thieves and thugs. In 1934 J. Edgar Hoover's G-men got permission to carry and use guns. Before the year was out, the law killed every one of these criminals. Gangsters and mobsters still went about their business, but small gangs and lone operators were less frequently encountered. The crooks and thugs still around were not the flamboyant, riveting characters that these earlier outlaws had been.

But in March 1939, a young Wyoming desperado blazed on the scene like a meteor. As a result of his crime spree, which began with an elk poach, seven men died, including the desperado himself. It was over in a matter of days. But it caught the nation's attention.

On March 13 near Cody, Wyoming, two game wardens stopped a car carrying Earl Durand, two teenaged friends, the father of one of the boys, and a trunkful of poached elk meat. As the car stopped,

Durand jumped out and ran off into the night, rifle in hand. That night marked the beginning of Durand's last eleven days. The next morning he shot a rancher's calf, cutting out the tenderloin and eating it. That same day Durand was caught, arrested, tried, sentenced, jailed. But two days later he broke out, taking a deputy sheriff as hostage and making him drive to Durand's parents' farm. There he shot and killed two law officers who came to arrest him again. A posse searched for Durand for four days fruitlessly.

After hiding in the wilds for six days Durand made his way to several neighbors' farms, gathering food and more weapons. Early on the morning of the tenth day, he forced an elderly farm couple to drive him to the Beartooth mountains nearby. Soon a posse led by Sheriff Frank Blackburn approached Durand's hideout. Two hangers-on—not official members of the posse—broke out and ran toward Durand with the idea of killing him. Durand killed them instead.

At the search's climax, a posse of a dozen hunting guides and outfitters—all skilled marksmen—and a detachment of Montana National Guardsmen armed with a howitzer and mortar headed toward Durand's mountain lair. A plane armed with tear-gas canisters and dynamite bombs flew low through the canyon ready to flush Earl out. But, Earl had skedaddled after stealing an old deputy sheriff's badge from one of the men he killed. Impersonating a posseman, he flagged down a car and hijacked it, taking the driver and passengers hostage. Earl demanded they take him to the nearby town of Powell. After dumping his hostages outside of Powell, he drove into town and robbed the First National Bank of Powell, terrorizing the customers and staff. Another man was killed in the melee. Making his way from the bank to the car, Durand was shot by a high school kid kneeling in the doorway of a gas station across the street. Crawling back inside, Durand pressed his own gun to his neck, fired, and met his end there on the floor. The date: March 24, 1939.

Earl Durand's last eleven days left families, neighbors, and friends bereft. Park County was grief-stricken. The effects of the horrors rippled through the community.

Dramatic, unexpected, and with something of the inevitable about them, Earl Durand's last days led editorialists to predict that the story would become part of the lore and history of the country.

The *Denver Post* described the events in literary terms: "The most imaginative creator of pulp melodrama never, in his wildest dreams, produced as wild a story as Durand lived in his last eleven days. If it had been portrayed on the screen, no one would have believed it could be real." The writer went on to say, "To the saga of the wild west will be added tales of the strange lonely life of a 26-year-old mountain Tarzan who came back to civilization for a spectacular, bizarre exit. ... Earl Durand ... is destined to become a topic of folklore." The *Cody Enterprise* struck the same theme: "The story will endure through future generations and will become a part of the saga of the west."

Like so many predictions editorialists make in the heat of the moment, this one did not come true. People in the vicinity kept their views and opinions about the episode to themselves, and for good reason. The events were unpleasant. People did not want to offend. Neighbors did not find them a fit topic for conversation. As a result, the story pretty much faded from memory.

Still, vestiges remained. For years Cody's Irma Hotel offered guests a souvenir local history newspaper. Each guest room at the Irma is named for a local notable, and the paper describes the life of each room's namesake. One is named for Frank Blackburn, the much-respected sheriff of Park County, of which Cody is the county seat. Blackburn was the man who chased Durand to his undoing; the souvenir paper told the story and displayed the bizarre letter Durand left for Blackburn.

IN 1973 I WAS A PROFESSOR at Webster College in St. Louis, Missouri. I taught a course called "The Outsider and the American Dream," in which students studied American culture and values from the point of view of outsiders and outlaws. The students read and discussed books about hoboes during the Depression, the lexicon of pickpockets, Henry David Thoreau's *Walden,* and a dozen other works—a typical multi-disciplinary American studies course. When we read some Zane Grey outlaw tales, a student said she knew a song that fit those stories' themes. At our next class, accompanying herself on the autoharp, she performed "The Ballad of Earl Durand"—another vestige of the story. A 1960s singer of classic folk songs wrote it, a fellow who called himself Charlie Brown. Brown performed it for Broadside Records in 1967 on a record called *Teton Tea Party*. The song's seven verses, refrain, and a narrative recited between verses depicted Durand as a man misunderstood. Claiming that Durand was "born too late a mountain man" and "in an earlier time he'd have been a mountain man," the song is sympathetic toward Durand and one-sided in his favor. It portrays Earl as a man hounded "by the law's bloodthirsty hand." Fascinated by the story the song tells (incorrectly), I then studied newspaper accounts of these 1939 events in the *Denver Post*, the *St. Louis Post-Dispatch*, and the *New York Times*. What actually happened was more interesting than the song's version of the story.

I wondered whether the people named in the newspaper reports might still live in the area, even forty years after Durand's spree of crime. The Cody and Powell telephone books confirmed my hunch. Several letters and phone calls later, I had arranged to interview some of the people who had taken part in the events. To see if the story was worth pursuing, in 1978 I took my wife and son to Cody to talk with the people, Ronnie Knopp among them. Sixteen at the time of Earl's spree, Ronnie was the young neighbor who perhaps knew him best. On a warm summer's evening our families met. (Ronnie's own son had never heard about Earl Durand and those days in his father's life.) Speaking freely, Ronnie talked about his friendship with Earl and what had happened to him during those eleven days.

When I turned the tape recorder off that evening, I could tell that if the other people I wanted to interview were as forthright and plainspoken as Ronnie was, I could recreate a rich piece of Wyoming history. As it turned out, they were. Between 1978 and 1981, I taped interviews with fourteen people in Cody and Powell and one in Billings, Montana, who played a role in the ordeal.

The hallmarks of historical writing are research, objectivity, and an accurate rendering of events and personalities. In writing of this kind, the author usually refers to the people in the account by name, or some designation, or with third-person pronouns: "he," "she," or "they." In this book's fifteen chapters, fifteen people who took part in the events describe their roles in what happened. Each speaks in the first person as "I." In this regard *The Last Eleven Days of Earl Durand* differs from most other accounts of actual events. Don't let the unusual form fool you; everything in this factual recreation really happened.

The fifteen speakers were not bystanders, observers, or mere commentators; they were participants. Nor was Earl an outsider; he was part of the community. He grew up in Powell. At the time of Earl's "bloody reign of terror" (as the *Denver Post* put it), the Durands were a well-known and respected family. Earl's father, Walter, was a successful farmer and a member of the Freemasons, having served as Worshipful Master of the Powell Lodge. Two of the Durand daughters were teachers at Powell High School. Mrs. Durand was well liked in the community. The family attended church every Sunday.

Eleven of the narrators I interviewed knew the Durands, knew Earl, or knew about him. Some were farmers and ranchers Earl had worked for. Some knew him as a generous neighbor who went out of his way to help in time of need. Three raps of a rifle butt against the front door, and they knew Earl was stopping by to say hello, see how they were doing. He was an infrequent but welcome visitor. Three of the people I interviewed knew him as teenagers and hunted or went "plinkin'"—target shooting—with Earl. Others belonged to the Heart Mountain Gun Club and shot and hunted with Earl, too. His neighbors knew that he spent the spring, summer, and fall roaming alone in the mountains and lived in a tent beside his family's house for the winter. Some had run into him in the backcountry or the mountains and saw Durand's disregard of the rules of backcountry life. Because they knew Earl, the people I interviewed had much to tell beyond the newspaper accounts.

Based on my initial research, I wrote the first draft in the manner of the typical history book—chronologically ordered and from the historian's perspective—to lay out the sequence of events clearly for myself. But when I interviewed Ronnie Knopp, I could tell that the book would work best in the voices of the narrators. The next few interviews convinced me that this was so. The spoken word—the phrasing of the accounts, the anecdotes specific to the way of life and, hence, to the personalities of the people, the flavor of place, and the texture of the time—gave life to the Durand story. You could say that the interviews are the "woof" for this book, with documentary information woven into the "warp." Most of the text and information comes straight from the interviews I taped, transcribed, and edited for clarity. The newspapers reported facts that none of the people I interviewed mentioned or knew. I worked this information into the spoken text to create the impression of seamless conversation. Thus, the reader sees the events, and the observations and opinions about them, from fifteen points of view.

Forty years is a long time to recall events that flew by in a flash. Nonetheless, what these people told me corresponded with the newspaper accounts. Even so, the newspapers made several errors, overstating the number of possemen, for example. In addition, while the *Denver Post* lavished the appellation "Tarzan of the Tetons" on Durand, he did not resemble Tarzan in any regard, and the events took place nearly two hundred miles away from the Teton mountains.

The area Durand had himself driven to is called the Beartooth Plateau of the Beartooth Range. People in the area often refer to locations by the name of the drainage rather than the individual mountain, most of which are unnamed. This was the Clarks Fork drainage. Newspapers reported the name of the mountain where Durand faced the posse variously as Sawtooth Mountain and Beartooth Mountain. For convenience, I call the mountain Beartooth in the book.

EARL DURAND WAS A MAN out of step with his time. The community in which he grew up was a model of its type and time. Modern farming methods supported by an exemplary irrigation system, up-to-date schools, churches, fine people and social institutions: all these surrounded him. But Durand's heart was in the mountains and in the ways of the mountain men. This bizarre, tragic history is a throwback to the clash of a bygone day between civilization and the wild man, a clash long gone by the late 1930s. Once these mountains had been a place where a man's own desires governed his actions. The law was his own sense of right, his will, and his gun. Out of this old world of history and folklore, tragedy and melodrama, arose Earl Durand, bringing to life for a moment the old conflict. He was an embodiment, a manifestation, an incarnation of the archetype of the mountain man at the edge of civilization. His last eleven days changed the course of many lives. The seven dead left behind wives, children, mothers and fathers, and friends to live through loss, disgrace, and anger. The Durands soon moved to Jackson Hole, a world away from Powell. Ronnie Knopp left home for the Northwest, not to speak with his family for many years. The events seasoned the lives of many. The sad events in Powell the night of Friday, March 24—hundreds of people visiting the bank, crowds clustering around the possemen to hear their stories, more than a thousand citizens passing through the Easton's Funeral Home to see the body of the badman Earl Durand—did not speak well of our morbid curiosity. Around Powell the story reverberates, now a faded memory to some, stories in bits and pieces for others, a legend of a time, of a place and its people.

THE POACH

Something of a hero, something of a joke in the
country around Powell, Wyoming was huge, shaggy
Earl Durand. From boyhood up, Earl talked about
wanting to be a "truewoodsman," a "Daniel Boone."

Time, March 27, 1939

Ronnie Knopp
Sixteen-Year-Old Poacher

MY FATHER AND STEPMOTHER moved the family from Montana to a farm just north of Powell, Wyoming, in September of 1938. We got there right in time for me to start school. During the first few weeks, I made friends with Tom Spint. He was in the same grade as me and we got off at the same bus stop. Tom walked west from the corner where the bus let us off and I turned north. But we lived close enough to each other so we could pal around together after school. A constant topic of our conversation was our neighbor Earl Durand.

Tom knew all kinds of stories about Earl and his unusual ways, the ways of a mountain man. He was a raw meat eater, a crack shot with any kind of firearm, slick at skinning, butchering, tanning hides, and all the old-time crafts of the West and the mountains. To tell the truth, half of it sounded like stuff Tom might have read about in Western story magazines, and he told it as if it was about Earl Durand. I was more than a little skeptical.

Though Tom was fun to pal with, he laid it on too thick about Earl Durand as far as I was concerned. I didn't want to be taken in like a stooge or a gullible farm boy, so I listened and tried to separate the wheat from the chaff. Besides, Tom was a little too bossy. When we got together, we usually ended up doing what he wanted to do, which was fun enough, but he wasn't too interested in taking up any of my suggestions. But this far out of town you had to make do with the companionship you could find. Since my brother, Ed, two years older than me, had moved to Gillette to work at the time the family moved to Powell, it was just me and the folks at home. So I was glad to have Tom to bum with.

The Durands were our nearest neighbors. We joined the church they belonged to, and Earl's sister Mildred was my math teacher. I was sixteen, a junior in high school. Earl was ten years older than me. Earl done an awful lot of walking every day—not only Earl, but Mildred as well. She would walk past our farm all the time, stop by and visit with my folks every now and then. Neighborly. Earl would walk by, too. I'd seen him several times at a distance, but he didn't stop. I was fascinated by Earl. Even from a distance, I could see he wore his hair clear down his shoulders and had a big beard. He usually wore a buckskin jacket and trousers and moccasins.

IT WAS ONE OF THOSE Indian summer November Saturdays. Tom and I were in the front yard playing catch. Down the road came Earl on one of his runs. He was well conditioned, full of stamina, full of vitality. He had a rifle slung over his back. I saw him first. "Boy, that's Earl Durand. Do you think you could get him to stop so I could meet him?" I asked. "Sure," Tom said, showing off that he knew Earl pretty well. He cupped his hands around his mouth and shouted, "Hey, Earl! I got a friend I'd like for you to meet." Earl came up to us. "Hello, boys," he said. "How you doing, Tom?" Then, turning to me he said, "And this young feller—I haven't met you yet. I'm Earl Durand. You just moved in, didn't you?"

"I'm Ronnie Knopp. Pleased to meet you."

We shook hands.

What Tom said about him could be true. I knew that time would tell. In a way it was like meeting somebody out of history, Daniel Boone or Davy Crockett or one of them mountain men we heard so much about. Around here everybody talked about Buffalo Bill Cody. Earl reminded me of Buffalo Bill in the days when he was a scout and a buffalo hunter. Earl was burly and strong, a big, husky bear of a man. Just from being up close to him, I could tell that he could take care of himself anywhere, get out of any scrape, stand up for his rights. Though I hadn't heard of him getting into any fights or brawls, I could tell that he'd be a match for any two ordinary men.

Earl said to me, "I'm staying in a sheepwagon up above your homestead, herding sheep for my old man. A while back I borrowed his car and drove it straight into the back of a truck. The entire radiator and the front end was pretty well wrecked up. I had the car towed to town and got it all fixed. To pay my father back for the repair bill, I'm herding his sheep." He laughed. "I ain't much for driving. I prefer horses or my own two feet. Them machines will be my downfall yet." Then he said, "You boys are welcome to come up and visit."

"When can we come?" I asked.

"Drop by this afternoon if you want," he said. "We'll take some guns and ammunition and go plinkin'." Then he said to me, "Toss your baseball up and let's see if I can hit it." I threw the ball as high as I could. Earl swung his rifle into place and let fire. He hit it four times. The ball jumped to a different place in the air each time. He was as good a shot as I'd ever seen. Earl laughed and asked, "Think you can put that baseball back together?" I picked up the shredded mess and just held it in my hand.

"Hardly what I'd call a baseball any more," I said.

"If it wasn't for that car accident, I sure as hell wouldn't be herding a flock of stupid sheep."

Just then my father called from the shed. "Ronnie, it's time to get to the barn and tend to the animals." Earl said, "Get along with you, kids. I hate farm work."

That very afternoon Tom and I headed up the road, walking side by side in the wheel ruts. All of a sudden, about fifty yards short of the sheepwagon, we heard two shots just like they were fired from an automatic rifle. Two clumps of dirt kicked up right between us. And, I mean, if we didn't stop flat in our tracks! We looked at each other. Did we want to run, turn and run? Or did we want to go on? We froze, we were so damn scared. I worried that Earl had taken a dislike to me or changed his mind about wanting us to visit. I had heard a lot about Earl, how unpredictable he was, how he wasn't what you might call completely civilized.

A sheepwagon door is divided in two, top and bottom—a Dutch door, they call it. The upper half flew open and Earl let out the damnedest, deepest laugh! So we didn't turn and run. We went up to the wagon. Earl said, "Hope I didn't scare you. I'm too good a shot to miss you if I'm aiming for you or hit you if I'm not. Come on in, boys."

He had a lot of rifles and pistols. In the wagon he kept rifle bullets by the gallon can and shotgun shells in water buckets. Tom and I, like all boys, loved hunting and shooting, but we couldn't afford ammunition. It was that way for almost everybody in those Depression days: no money, let alone money for extras. "That paint can is level full," Earl said. "Take a handful of bullets each and we'll walk up in the hills, do a little plinkin'." We each dug in. "Fill your pockets," he said. "There's plenty."

As we walked toward the hills I asked, "What was that rifle you were shooting? Automatic?"

"Hell, no. It wasn't no automatic."

Tom said, "Then it must have been a repeater."

"Not a repeater either." He handed the rifle over and showed it to us. "It's just this old single shot."

I said, "I don't believe it. Nobody can work the bolt, drop in another shell, and fire again so quick."

"See them two dead limbs on that tree?" he asked, pointing out a cottonwood about thirty-five yards down the trail.

Without another word Earl took back his rifle, dipped two shells out of his pocket, and fired. First the lower limb fell, shattered close to the trunk. A second later the one above, longer and thicker, came crashing to the ground. I learned why Earl had a reputation as one of the best shots in Wyoming: he was a hell of a shot.

From then on Tom and I did a lot of plinkin' with Earl. We'd poke through the dumps around town and hunt up the smallest little perfume bottles. Earl would toss one up, grab his rifle, and shoot that bottle to shards and splinters, knock it right out of the air. He'd never miss. "It's easy once you get the hang of it," Earl said. He blasted away at another Lilac Perfume bottle. "Whatever you're throwing, you catch the target at the top. For an instant the target's not rising and not falling. You shoot at a steady target." It's one of those tricks that the audience always applauds. Buffalo Bill was a master of it. Exhibition marksmen from Winchester and Remington are good at it, too.

One day we were rummaging around a dump in a dry gully. "Find me all the little Carnation condensed milk cans around," Earl said. Tom and I scared up about half a dozen. "I'll tell you the trick.

You each take one in each hand and hold them out to your sides at arm's length."

"Are you crazy?" Tom shouted. "Count me out." He ran over to an old couch and sat down on its broken springs as if to say "I won't budge on this one."

"You don't trust me? You don't think I can hit 'em?" Earl asked.

"I don't intend to find out."

"How 'bout you, Knopp?"

"Okay." I was confident of his ability.

Earl had me hold the can out from my side, with the bottom end facing him. The bottom of a condensed milk can has one circle inside another like a target. Earl backed off thirty-five paces, then shot the center circle right out. He shot half a dozen cans right out of my fingers.

Earl only had an inch either way before he'd hit my hand. But he never hit me. I wouldn't hold like that for anyone else, that's for sure. Come to think of it, it was plenty crazy in the first place.

FROM THEN ON IT WAS A rare night when I didn't go visit the mountain man. Tom would come along sometimes, but he always acted like a kid. He always wanted to do the talking. I wasn't interested much in what Tom had to say. He would brag and lie right to Earl's face. I was interested in what Earl had to say. Earl and I soon became fast friends. In October he moved out of the sheepwagon and into a good-sized tent behind his folks' house. Every evening we'd talk and Earl would tell me about his adventures, his upbringing. We spent so much time together it didn't take long for me to learn nearly everything there was to know about Earl. Earl had three sisters, all grown. His folks were pretty well along in years when he was born. Earl told me he figured his mother didn't want a boy. She thought a boy would be too much trouble at her age. She was right. "For a long time I didn't like my mother. She curled my hair in long ringlets until I was six," Earl remembered. She dressed him in lace and dresses well beyond the age for which the style was fashionable. "I despised the clothes and long hair. That was what our first fights were over," Earl said with disgust. "She dressed me fit to go to Sunday school during my first years of school."

Earl Durand lived in this tent behind his parent's home part of the year.
(AP/Wide World Photos)

Strangely enough, long hair is what he came to prefer. He copied the mountain men—Jim Bridger, Kit Carson, and, most of all, our local legend, Codyite of world renown, Buffalo Bill. Earl had long hair almost up to his last day. Cutting it and shaving off his beard made it hard for the posse to know exactly what Earl looked like when it came time for them to search for him.

He caught pneumonia at twelve or thirteen, double pneumonia. He nearly died. He was bedridden for several months, and when he got better he was very weak. The doctor encouraged him to exercise a little each day and increase it until he regained his strength. Soon he was running long distances, building up his stamina, doing chin-ups and lifting dumbbells. When spring came, he began sleeping outdoors in his bedroll. Then he started going off by himself. At first he went only as far as Polecat Bench, a sharp rise of land that flattens into a broad, long tabletop, just west of Powell.

Soon Earl was away for weekends at a time, hiking all over the flats, the Bench, and up into the hills and mountains. The first winter after his illness, he slept with his bedroom window open, and the next winter he built himself a sturdy canvas house, a tent held taut by a frame of two-by-fours. Earl recovered completely and kept on going. He ranged farther and farther and stayed away longer. By the time he was sixteen, he was gone from April to September or October—kept himself alive with a knife, a gun, and his wits.

When he was eighteen, Earl had a second brush with death. He was crawling through the strands of a barbed-wire fence, his gun cradled in one arm. The trigger hung up on something, and Earl shot himself through the chest. Three weeks later he was out on his treks again. Tremendously strong fellow. Earl could easily walk forty miles a day through the most rugged terrain. His marksmanship was legendary. Anyone who hunted or went plinkin' with him saw bullets, arrows, knives—whatever he was hunting with—fly to their marks as if Earl controlled their path with his thoughts. There was something uncanny about his abilities.

All us boys were naturally expected to work on the farms from spring through autumn, dawn till night, plowing, planting, and hoeing until harvest was done and the crops hauled to market. So there were arguments in the Durand household between Earl and his family about his uncooperative ways.

Earl didn't get along with his dad. It was mutual. They didn't have any love for each other. Walter Durand was pretty old to be doing all the farm work himself. He had every right to expect a certain amount of work from his strapping son, but Earl was a mountain man and wouldn't have hardly anything to do with farming and chores. During the time of the year when his family needed him most, he was off on his treks. In the spring of the year, Earl's sister Mildred would drive him up to the mountains. With his pack and shells and gun, he would be gone practically all summer.

There were family rows, and I can understand the family's point. Up till then I would have been ashamed to even think that I wasn't going to do exactly what my father told me when it came to farm work and chores. Of course, I changed my ways soon, too—became more like Earl. But I had to, more or less.

Since he was a kid Earl had known all the guides, cowboys, and outfitters working in this part of Wyoming. It didn't take long for the young woodsman to know every inch of the Big Horns, the Beartooths, the Yellowstones, Absarokas, and Tetons, each one an awesome range in itself, difficult to master, each the home of a different Spirit. For the rest of his life Earl lived half the year alone in these mountains, which started within view of his home and stretched for hundreds of miles in three directions. From the marrow up Earl was made of the mountains. By the time he recovered from his battle with pneumonia, he'd grown into a bear of a man. And like all the boys who grew up in this part of the country, he was fascinated by stories of the mountain men who had roamed the untouched stretches of territory. Six foot two, a hundred and ninety pounds, and tough as a grizzly, Earl already walked the path that would lead his life to resemble theirs—but in the wrong place, you might say, and at the wrong time.

Earl preferred to be by himself. At the same time he was awful friendly. Many's the neighbor he helped with chores or repairs. He mixed with crowds down at the gravel pits for skating. He loved to skate, cutting the ice like an eagle skimming on the wind.

On hunting parties he always killed the most game. In the Depression the land fed a lot of people here. During hunting season, game made up a good part of our diet. The old plainsmen and the Indians hunted all the time. Earl did, too. When he was in the mountains he hunted for his food, license or no license. But in the days of "No Hunting" signs and licenses, that was called poaching. Earl poached even when he was living at his folks' place. This was another subject of their disagreement. Earl killed game for the poor, for widows with orphans. He dressed it for them and was invited to many a dinner at the homes of the people he fed.

I learned a lot about hunting from Earl. Everyone except him hunted rabbits with a shotgun. He hunted them with a rifle. He said, "I don't like picking buckshot out from between my teeth." He taught me to hunt them with a rifle, too. Once in a while Earl's father would lend him the car, and we'd drive up to an old abandoned coal mine. He discovered a great spot no one else knew about. We'd hunt for an afternoon and bring back a couple dozen rabbits. We poached pheasants all the time. Earl would shoot pheasants right out of the air with his rifle. With his teaching I soon got to where I could shoot pheasants with a .22 just like he did. It's just practice. In those days there really wasn't much of a game warden problem.

EARL AND I NOTICED WE had kind of drifted away from Tom, so we decided to have a day of fishing, the three of us together. As it turned out, that day widened the rift between Tom and us.

To start it was just a good old time. Earl was taking us up to Deep Lake, on a slope of Beartooth Plateau, the same mountain Earl picked later to face off against the posse. Me and Tom had backpacks to carry the fish, but no poles, hooks, lines, or bait. On the way up we stopped at a coal mine north of town. Earl told the mine boss, "I need a dozen sticks of dynamite and six detonators. We're going fishing." The man sold us all we wanted. "Give us some fish on the way down if you get any," he said.

Earl carried the explosives in his pack. As we hiked up the mountain, I got to thinking about those men from California and Chicago and the East, the men who called themselves hunters, fishermen, or sportsmen. We didn't think of ourselves that way. But those men hired guides. I asked Earl, "Did you ever think of being a guide?"

He snorted. "My life is the mountains. I'm not here to entertain the rich." Earl liked stories of how folks got by, how they did things for themselves. He encouraged us to spin yarns, not old-timey stuff, or boasting like the men in town gave out, but things that had actually happened to us. While we were climbing he asked, "Did either of you ever fish with dynamite before?"

Right away I thought of some sparkling early-winter nights in Montana. I said, "In Montana our farm was a few miles from a lake. In the winter when the ice was right, not frozen in the middle yet, the ranchers met at the lake with a bunch of us kids. We circled the lake, each man fifty feet away from the next to start, and edged out onto the ice. Then we hit the ice with shovels, sticks, poles, and us kids just tromped on it. The idea was to herd the fish into the center of the lake. We kept moving toward that hole of water, slowly getting closer to each other. When we got close enough, one of the ranchers lit the fuse and lowered a bundle of dynamite into the water. Before the fuse burned down and the dynamite exploded, we all ran as far as we could, a bunch of ranchers and kids slipping and sliding, yippeein' and whoopin', laughing and having the time of our lives. The dynamite never even touched the fish; the concussion alone killed them. After the explosion the fish surfaced. Then we crept to the edge of the ice, reached out into the water with nets and pitchforks, and harvested the fish into gunny sacks like ears of corn, some of them still flopping around. There was a big fish fry late into the evening, and we cached the rest to eat the next few days. It was a way of restocking the larders."

We walked and talked. By now we had passed the timberline. We still had a ways to go.

Earl asked, "What about you, Tom? Did you do any fishing that would surprise the sportsmen?"

Tom said, "This part of the country is famous for its canals bringing the Shoshone River down to irrigate the Bighorn Basin. A lot of catfish and buffalo fish make an easy living in those canals. In the summer when you were gone, Earl, the farm hands dammed one end of a canal and diverted the water. They built a weir to trap the fish where the water ran out. And when the water drained out, them cowboys got in the mud wearing rubber buckle-up galoshes and went to work with pitchforks, harvesting fish like pitching hay. There was big fish barbecues and smokes."

Earl liked stories. Jawin', he called it. We swapped some more and pretty soon we reached the lake.

Tom was always looking for excuses to get what he considered the glamour jobs. First he wanted to be the one who tied the detonators to the dynamite. Just as Earl was getting ready to rig, Tom piped up, "Hey, Earl, let me be the one in charge of explosives. I know how to do it."

"No, Tom, that's my job."

Tom started whining and arguing. "Come on, Earl. Let me. I come up the mountain for some fun. Now are you gonna let me?" He thought he was in charge, but he wasn't at all. Earl just glowered. So Tom turned on me and said, "Well, at least let me do all the tossing," trying to get a rise out of me, which he did.

"Oh, no, you don't!" I said, and stood up to let him know I wasn't going for his bratty ways either.

He said, "You light 'em and I'll heave 'em."

To tell the truth, up till then it didn't make the slightest difference to me what I did, but his snooty manner raised my ire, and I wasn't going to cooperate with him at all. I said, "I'll take turns with you."

"Take turns, nothing!" Tom said. "I ain't a little kid. Take turns! You and Earl are together all the time. Now that I'm here, I want a chance to do something." He jumped up, ran over to me, and started scuffling just like a little kid on the playground at recess. I was stunned and just let swing with a roundhouse punch to his nose. Blood started pouring out. I could tell it was one of those punches that feels like a rubber mallet hitting you because the tears welled up in his eyes and flowed without his crying. It took the pep right out of him.

Earl rigged two of the dynamite sticks with a detonator and tied them to a rock. When he finished making four of these, he said, "Let's go fishing!" and lit the fuses. Tom and I took turns tossing the bundles into the lake. I went first. Then there'd be an explosion and the water would boil. As it turned out there were no fish in Deep Lake. For the dozen sticks we set off, we got only about half a dozen fish. Earl said, "Maybe they're spawning. We'll hunt for them on the way down."

We hiked down the mountain from the lake and crossed a stream. There were all the fish. They were so big, their fins stuck out of the water. "We'll divert the stream with rocks," Earl said. We just scooped out a haul of fish below the diversion. When we got all we could carry, we pulled out the rocks and let the stream go back about its business. Earl said, "There'll be a lot of roe in the females. I like it dipped in cornmeal and fried in butter."

Tom was sore the rest of the day. I could tell that Earl thought less of Tom than before. Instead of the rift between us shrinking, it grew wider. I still liked Tom some, but not much.

We weren't even thinking about game wardens or licenses for fishing or hunting. Nobody was. Not in those days. We hunted pheasants and ducks all winter long around home and never gave a thought to a license. But game wardens—that's just where we made our mistake. Earl hunted or went plinkin' with almost everyone in town. He was a member of the Heart Mountain Rod and Gun Club. He shot with those guys now and then. But the year I knew him, he spent the most time with me. I lived closest by and visited him as often as I could. Many an evening I spent in his tent that winter. Me and sometimes Tom. Earl kept a kerosene stove burning in his tent to keep the cold off in the winter, and you got used to the chill after a while. Tom came by once in a while. He always acted like we didn't want him there, but he was just behaving so spiteful and snooty that it was all we could do just to tolerate him.

When Durand got with other people he wouldn't talk much. But when kids were around, he was a hell of a good visitor. He read a lot. Western magazines. And he knew everything about the most famous outlaw band ever to ride the trail, the "Wild Bunch,"—Kid Curry, Butch Cassidy, Harry Tracy. Before it was over, the newspapers would call Earl "the worst killer since Kid Curry." He knew all about their stronghold, called the Hole in the Wall, over by Buffalo. He spent some time over there. He told me about his outings and how he lived off the land.

Once he told me about his trip to New Mexico. "I wanted to see if I could live like the mountaineers, taking off and going great distances on horseback. I was trying out the old ways of doing things, to see if they really worked. I was crossing the desert and some Indians jumped me. They took every bit of my money, everything I had, except twenty-one dollars I had stashed in my clothes. I went to the nearest town, bought myself a pistol. Needless to say, I got back everything the Indians took from me and then some."

"What do you mean?" I asked. But Earl didn't elaborate any further, and I didn't ask him any more questions about it. I knew better than to pry. It wouldn't do any good. Earl was willing to say what he was willing to say, and beyond that, don't ask. That was how he was.

He taught me a lot about the ways of the badman, the Indians, and the mountain men. He read a lot about these subjects in Western magazines, but mostly he learned from living the life of a mountaineer for half the year from the age of sixteen on.

Often I'd stay in Earl's tent while he ran, reading his Western magazines—he had a couple of stacks of them, each about two feet high. Every evening he would run the four miles that go around the section, the square mile my family lived on. All the farmers around the section kept dogs, and on a still night I could hear them bark as Earl went past. I could track him all the way around by the sound of the dogs barking.

One night I was absorbed in a Max Brand story. Suddenly I heard Earl's voice.

"Good story?"

I hadn't heard him come in or anything. "I didn't know you were there, Earl."

"Stalkin'. I'll teach you how to do it. I could sneak up on you any time and you'd never know I was there."

After that Earl practiced stalking and such with me. "Tomorrow night when you come, see if you can sneak up on me," Earl said. I made every effort to be quiet so that Earl wouldn't know I was there. I always went there after dark, being it was winter and after supper. But every time, Earl would hear me from a distance, sneak out of the tent, and come up behind *me*, his senses were so sharp. "I'm training you in valuable skills," he told me.

One night Earl taught me another move. He handed me an empty pistol and said, "Come up behind me just like you're sticking me up." I did what he told me to do. But as he raised his hands, he turned just a tiny bit and with his elbow he knocked the gun away from his back. He whirled around so fast, his arm hit me and knocked me flat. He was quick. We only practiced that one a couple of times. It hurt to get hit that hard, so we quit doing it.

We talked away many an evening after Earl got back from his running. Earl knew so much about the ways of the West—hunting, trapping, stalking game. He had from spring through autumn to try out and perfect what he learned. He had all the time a guy could want to learn the ways of wildlife.

He had great hunting adventures, as good as the ones in the magazines. One night he told me, "I once joined a herd of bighorn sheep." I asked, "What do you mean?"

"One summer I spent a couple of months as high as you'd ever want to get in the mountains traveling with a herd of bighorns."

I was mystified. "I still don't get it, Earl."

"I watched them for a while, then mimicked their movements." Earl got up and showed me. "Instead of walking directly up to them, I meandered about, hunched over, looking down at the ground, as if I was weak. I had watched the rest of the herd submit to the leader, including the rams. They all gave in to the leader." Then he stood up tall and walked around the tent. "If I had approached the herd standing, walking straight toward them and looking them in the eye, they would have taken off when I was still a hundred years away. Every hunter sees them bolt and disappear that way."

"Were you surprised that they just stayed where they were?"

"No, they just nibbled at the tufts of scrub and grass and glanced in my direction every few seconds."

"Where did you learn this?"

"Just by watching and trying it out. I did it for several hours one afternoon, found the herd again the next morning, and stayed with them for a few days. On the fourth day the leader charged at me, brushing my left hand as he swerved by. The leader had accepted me as a member of the herd, he let me visit whenever I wanted. I passed many a day with them, wandering with them through the high country of the Beartooths. Once when a sudden summer blizzard hit, I set myself up under a low overhang. When I got scrunched down out of the snow and wind, the leader came in and snuggled up against me. The rest of the herd—females, kids, and unattached rams—also made their way in. For several hours there was nothing but their bleatings and smoke of breathing and me watching."

If Earl had had a more scientific bent, he would have made a great naturalist.

Earl also knew a lot about the ways of the Indian. He learned to hunt the ways they did. He studied the wildlife so closely he knew pretty well when a herd of elk would come down to a salt lick or stream or browse in a particular meadow. "I can teach you how to track a deer all day without the animal ever knowing you're near" he'd say. Many a time Earl told me, "In order to hunt, you have to put yourself in the mind of the prey." He perfected the art. He'd always bag the most game of anyone on a hunt. He also cooked like an Indian, smoking meat and jerking venison, though he preferred his meat raw. Earl could snare and trap small game. He could spot animals at a distance. He knew their nesting places. Earl could read their scat and tracks. He knew how to use herbs and plants for medicine and healing. Durand knew the constellations of the zodiac, the planets, weather signs.

Once Earl and I went out on a two-day hunt. I carried my bedroll, pots, grub, and rain gear. It got cold in the mountains at night in almost all seasons. First we hunted on Cedar Mountain where Earl caught us two rabbits, then skinned, split, and roasted them over the coals of a small fire for dinner. Earl wasn't completely opposed to eating meat cooked, he just preferred it raw. Then by the light of the full moon we climbed down Cedar, crossed the road and started up the Rattlesnake. As we hiked, Earl talked about the Indians. He was as interested in their ways as he was in Daniel Boone and the mountain men. For one thing, the mountain men just took on Indian ways and added what they knew as white men. But Earl's main interest was in Indian religion. I couldn't tell if he actually knew any Indians or only read or heard about them. Maybe he made up all he told me about the medicine man and sacred places, medicine bundles and all that. But as we hiked up the river, he told me we were going to a sacred spot and I needed to act like I was in church. He told me after this night I would understand life a little better, and I could return to the spot on my own to draw on its power.

We scrambled over boulders clear up to the foot of a vertical face, about as high as you could get climbing from the direction we started. There are a lot of sheer cliffs in the mountains hereabouts, but the Palisade is the tallest and longest mountain face near town. Earl said, "You'll know the place when you find it. It's nothing out of the ordinary you'll notice. In fact, when you find it, like I did, you'll say, 'Of course this is the place.' Now look."

Look? All there was was the light of the moon. Look for what? But I went along with it. Earl pointed to the rock face, motioned with his hand uphill a little. So I angled in that direction, made my way to the cliff, and followed the boulders at its foot. The sky was cloudless, and on nights like this the wind blows in the mountains and the temperature drops way down. After I went about fifty yards, I came upon a pharaoh's throne right on the mountainside. I had seen pictures in schoolbooks of statues of pharaohs carved right into mountains. They were sitting on their thrones and looking out over the Nile River. The back of this one right in front of me must have gone up about two hundred feet to the clear sky. The seat of it started just about eye level and was about five feet wide. And up about two feet from the seat was an arm on each side. I said, "This is the spot."

Earl said, "I told you you'd recognize it. Scramble up. I'll toss you your bedroll. That's where you'll be tonight." He told me to watch the movement of the heavens through one night so I could appreciate, just for its own sake, the majesty of the universe. Earl put it so nice, I could tell he was speaking his heart.

I stayed awake most of the night, dozing off once in a while, then waking when Earl spoke to me.

"Rattlesnakes and antelope are gods. You must never kill them or if you do, you'll soon die. But all the other animals are made for man to use. They belong to any man who can kill them." He talked along in that vein most of the night. All this time I was lying on the cold stone ledge, looking up to the west watching the stars wheel. It seemed like every time I looked to where the rock cut off the sky, I saw a new star crossing into view. The stars travel like the sun, east to west. I realized how fast the earth spins. Several times that night I had the feeling that the earth was dumping me off my narrow perch. It was the strangest sensation, like you feel when you stop on top of the ferris wheel and rock your seat.

I saw the Great Bear roaming the sky, tracking west with the hunter chasing him. Earl said, "Orion and the bear is the story of mankind until the discovery of farming." Earl hated farming and loved hunting. He told me that those early ideas about spirits in the form of animals, places, rocks and such had a lot of truth to them. He said he learned a way of hunting from an Indian—how to become the prey, communicate with the animal's spirit, tell it that you needed food and that the time for its life to end had arrived. Maybe there was something to what Earl said. He was always the guy who brought home the most meat.

I never got to speak with Earl about the medicine man or Indian ways again.

When you get right down to it, the night on the Rattlesnake wasn't nothing unusual, and at the same time it changed me. Over the years I got a lot of good out of going to that spot. Sometimes just to look at it now puts me at peace. Orion hunting the bear. Earl, the great hunter, who later became the Great Bear himself. Maybe it was as simple as that.

EARL STUDIED A LOT FROM correspondence courses he mail-ordered from the magazines he bought. He taught himself gun repair, locksmithing, and a slew of other skills. He kept his firearms in tiptop shape. He liked working in his father's tool shed. Earl also bought liniments and salves through the mail. He loved looking through catalogues, ordered near every one he could find.

We talked about guns and hunting a lot. One evening he went to a wooden box in the corner of his tent and took out a huge pistol. "I always carry two guns, a .357 Magnum pistol and a little .22. Last year when I went to the mountains for the summer I didn't take a rifle, I just took this Magnum." He took out an oiled cloth and cleaned the gun as he talked.

"It gave me both hands free. I shot whatever I needed—a deer, an elk. I'd get a bear bothering me, every once in a while a grizzly, and I'd kill it with my Magnum. I'd cut the claws out and keep them." Earl got up and took a small leather pouch out of his trunk, then sat down again across from me. He handed me the pouch and said, "Open it. It's yours." It was a bagful of claws. At moments like that I felt that Earl had accepted me as a kind of apprentice, you might say. He had a lot to teach me.

Earl kept his .22 pistol in a shoulder holster. He'd never be without it, but no one ever knew he was carrying it.

Folks used to ice skate at a gravel pit two miles east of Powell. Earl and I were both good skaters. You know how cattails fuzz out in the winter? Well, Earl snapped off a stalk and the head with it. He chased me with it. I dodged and turned, but Earl kept close. Finally he caught up with me and thumped me on the head with that doggone cattail. I was just covered with fuzz. So naturally I tried to do the same thing back at him. I grabbed myself a cattail and was skating as hard as I could, waving that stalk, getting ready to thump Earl back. I was drawing pretty close to him and he whips out his doggone pistol and shoots the head right off the stalk, and I got showered with fuzz a second time. He laughed! He had the deepest laugh. I saw the humor in it, too. I didn't pick up another one, I can assure you.

Somehow I wound up with that little .22 pistol. I still have it. I must have put it someplace separate from the other rifles and guns I cached for him after he landed in jail.

ONE NIGHT IN THE MIDDLE of March I was sitting by Earl's little kerosene stove reading from a Western magazine by the light of a lamp and talking with Tom while Earl was out running. Tom still stopped by once in a while, even though he had longer to walk than I did, and his parents objected somewhat to his being with Earl. They thought he was a bad influence.

When Earl came in he sat down between us on the tent floor.

"I need to get some meat for a hungry family and my father won't let me use his car," he said. "He won't have anything to do with poaching, won't even let my mother cook any of the meat I bring in." He turned to me. "I need your father to take us up on the North Fork. We'll take Spint along and bag us some elk. I know you boys are on spring vacation from school the start of this week, and this would be a good time to go."

"My father doesn't like poaching any more than yours does," I said. "I don't think he'll do it. You might as well save your breath."

"Never mind that. I'll come over and talk him into it. In the meantime, put in a good word for me. There's some hungry folks up on Polecat Bench I aim to feed. We'll get him to take us."

That Saturday evening, March eleventh it was, my family had just finished dinner and my stepmother was clearing the table. There was a knock at the door. I answered it. It was Earl. "Come in," I said. Then I called to my father. "It's Earl Durand. I told you he might come over."

My father had a look of concern. He had never met Earl and he wasn't looking forward to meeting him now. My father had an opinion about Earl. Occasionally Earl would be mentioned at gatherings—church or the Grange or someplace like that. Not every-thing he had heard was bad. Earl helped out a lot of people, but he had strange ways and some ways that were questionable, like poaching. Since I had told Dad why Earl was coming, he was lean-ing in the direction of having a bad time of it with him. But he started out giving Earl a chance to put his best foot forward. That didn't last for long.

"Pleased to meet you, Mr. Knopp, Mrs. Knopp," Earl said. "Hope I'm not interrupting dinner. I can come back later."

"No, we're finished," Dad said. "Come in, Durand. Ronnie told me you wanted me to take you poaching. I can't."

"Yes, sir."

Dad began lecturing Earl. "I'm a religious, law-abiding man and I'm raising my sons to be the same. I like to hunt, but in season and with a license. But I won't take you poaching." Earl said, "I'm not asking you to hunt. There's a family in a bad way."

"It's the same difference—poach or take you poaching."

"I'm not going to sell the meat or anything like that, Mr. Knopp. It's a widow's family. People going hungry and the Lord's bounty all around."

"I know, but the law's the law."

Then Earl quoted Scripture at Dad. He said, "In the Good Book doesn't it say, 'And let them have dominion over the fish of the sea, and over the fowl of the air, and over the beasts of the field, and over all the earth?'" Like everyone else around here, Dad hated to see people suffer, the way folks did during the Depression. Some people were so hard up, they were leaving home. While we lived a little north of the usual route, we knew of a lot of people driving through the basin from the Midwest, on their way to California. You could almost see those thoughts going through my father's mind. "Well…" he muttered.

Earl jumped at the chance. "Just this once. I won't ask again. If we leave out early Monday morning, we'll be home by early evening. I'll help you with chores. I'll come by and help with any extra work you have."

"Aw, nuts." Dad was being badgered to death. "I don't like it one bit, but I'll take you this one time. But don't ask me again!"

"Okay," Earl said softly. He knew he had won his point and let it go at that. "I'll leave you folks to finish your dinner. Good night. I'll see you day after tomorrow."

EVERY CARLOAD OF TOURISTS or migrants that passes through Cody headed west to Yellowstone National Park drives along the North Fork River. There, against a background of towering mountains, they see fantastic wind-carved sandstone spires, needles, chimneys, and balancing rocks beside the road. How the river got its name— all the streams and creeks in this valley drain into the north fork of the Shoshone River. It flows through a mountain range named the Absarokas—pronounced "Absorkas" hereabouts. The North Fork is thick with game: bear, elk, deer, and the like. That area is where we were going.

Dad and I drove off that morning right after breakfast, picked up Earl, then Tom. Earl took charge. Late in the morning we reached the spot he had in mind. "As soon as we cross Suet Creek you'll see an overgrown logging road. Turn off there to the left." We drove up a lightly rutted path, went about a hundred yards into the woods, and stopped. You couldn't see the car from the main road. It looked like nobody had been on this road in years.

We got out and Earl gave directions. "Tom, follow the creek till you come to a meadow. Stay inside the woods. You ought to see some elk browsing in brush to the north. I'm going to a salt lick alongside a little spring up above here." He turned to me and said, "Ronnie, when you hear gunshots, come on. You'll dress the meat. Mr. Knopp, you just stay here at the car." In practically no time I heard gunfire from the direction Earl had gone. Before I even got to Earl, I heard Tom's rifle. Earl had shot a bull elk. Like you're supposed to do, before I knelt down to dress the meat I looked around. I caught a glimpse of a wisp of smoke rising from a chimney up the slope and over some treetops.

"Look, Earl." I pointed. "There's a cabin up there."

Earl looked. "Goddam! Somebody built it since I was up here last." It was rare for Earl to cuss. But he was angry, mostly at himself. He didn't like to be outsmarted. Worse yet, he didn't like to outsmart himself. He knew better than to hunt without looking around first. I had spotted the cabin by doing what Earl had taught me to do—and he hadn't done it himself. That's what irked him. He said, "Somebody's up there. He heard our guns. Whoever's up there might not like us taking this elk. He might have a two-way radio, too. You run over to Tom and bring him back to the car. We'll find a different spot."

We both took off on the run and stopped by my father at the car. Earl said, "We're taking off as soon as Ronnie brings in Spint."

"Where is the meat?"

"We're going someplace else."

"What'll we do about the meat? You aren't gonna leave two elk, are you? We can't just leave the meat."

"Quit arguing and do what I tell you, dammit," Earl growled.

My father didn't like this jaunt to begin with. He was nervous, afraid that his worst fears would come true. "Earl, either dress the meat and load it up or we're going home empty-handed. I'm not taking you any farther."

Earl's jaw tightened and his eyes narrowed. "Leave it. We'll find plenty more. We're getting out of here. There's other good spots." It was like a cloud had crossed Earl's face. "Don't make me madder than I am," he said. "Now get in the car and do what I say."

Dad could see that Earl meant business.

Earl took us to a second place ten miles or so farther west. As we were getting out of the car, Dad glanced at the gas gauge and said nervously, "I don't have enough gas to get back to Powell."

"You hold on, now," said Earl. He took a good look at the gauge himself before he said, "There's a gas pump back at the Half Moon Lounge. Drive there, fill up, and come right back. And no monkey business. You're in this as deep as me now. We'll shoot a couple more elk and have the meat dressed out and ready to go by the time you get back here."

In those days, while a man might hunt on his own property whenever he wanted, he sure wasn't going to let a stranger shoot game on his land or put up with someone poaching on National Forest. The person living in that cabin had radioed the game warden's office in Cody and reported shooting. Two game wardens, Boyd Bennion and Dwight King—who were with these events from the start to the finish—had driven through the rock-cut tunnel that bores through the southern tip of Rattlesnake Mountain about six miles west of Cody. Traveling east, just before the tunnel was Martin Craig's Half Moon Lounge and Restaurant, with a couple of gas pumps right alongside. The officers parked there because cars need to slow down before they enter the tunnel. They pulled in alongside the gas pumps.

Bennion told Dwight King, "Go across the road and flag the cars over to here. There ain't much traffic on this road headed east this time of year, so whoever comes through, flag 'em down and send 'em over." Soon my father drove up. He parked at the pump, got out of the car, and headed toward the door to find someone to pump the gas. Bennion came over behind Dad. Dad was as nervous as he could be but worked awful hard not to show it. "I need gas," was all he said. All he could think of was how lucky we hadn't loaded up the elk meat.

"I guess the joint's locked up," said Bennion. While they were talking, the warden looked Dad over and glimpsed inside the car. He could tell that Dad wasn't a poacher. All the telltale signs were missing. "The nearest place that's open is Bill Garlow's station on the near side of town." Garlow's mother was Buffalo Bill Cody's daughter, so Garlow was Buffalo Bill's grandson. "It's about five or six miles. Got enough gas to make it?"

"I think so. I'm pretty sure."

"Where you headed?"

"Powell. Thanks for the information."

"You're welcome."

Bennion walked back to his car. He told King, "He ain't the poacher."

Dad got back in his car and drove off toward Cody to buy gas. He was shaken.

It took him a while to get back to us in the woods. Earl and Tom had each killed another elk, and I just as quick dressed them. We all pitched in. Dad was more upset than I had ever seen him, worried. He was afraid of getting caught. He said, "I had a run-in with some game wardens. They got a call about those first two elk you shot. We're heading home. I'm not gonna tangle with the law. I was afraid something like this might happen. Forget the damn meat," he said with disgust. "We're going."

"What happened?" asked Earl.

"The wardens were parked up to the Half Moon. One came over and looked in the car. Don't even put the meat in the trunk, Earl. I'm sure they're stopping everybody. I'm letting you off up at the canyon. You'll have to walk home from there."

Earl turned downright nasty, like I had never seen him. "Hell, no!" he shouted. "The wardens already saw your car and know there ain't nothing in it. It'll be dark by the time we get to Cody. The boys and me will duck down out of sight. The wardens won't give us no trouble at all."

"They'll be checking every car that comes through. Besides, if they recognize my car, they'll know something's wrong. I told them I was going to Powell."

Earl didn't even bother to answer. He said, "Let's get going. Give me the keys. That meat's going in the trunk. I don't want any trouble from you. There's folks to feed and here's the meat ready to go." Earl didn't threaten Dad, but there was threat in his voice. He was working himself up into a fury.

Scared, Dad handed over the keys. "I don't like this one bit. This is gonna land us in trouble. I feel it coming." Us boys kept quiet and out of sight. Earl had us load the shoulders and loins wrapped in oiled paper. We discarded the ribs and neck. They don't have much meat to them. After we cached the two elk in the car trunk, we cleaned our guns and stashed them in canvas rifle cases alongside the meat. All except Earl. He carried his across his lap.

THE NORTH FORK ROAD has no shoulder. An old post-and-cable barrier fence is all that separates the road from the steep rocky bank that falls away to the river a dozen yards below. The tunnel's so narrow, many's the fender that comes through with paint scratched off. Folks have to slow down when they drive through. Just past dusk the lights of our car came into the wardens' view—Bennion and Dwight King were still parked at the tunnel entrance. Bennion turned on his headlights and the two of them hopped out, signaling with their flashlights for us to pull over and stop. Earl was in the front seat. He saw what was happening up ahead. He shouted, "Don't stop! Don't stop! Go faster! You can get past them!"

But Dad slowed down just enough so Boyd Bennion was able to jump on the running board and grab the door handle. He pulled out his revolver and aimed it at Dad's head. "Stop or I'll shoot!" he shouted.

Dad slammed on the brakes. He almost threw Bennion off the running board, he stopped so short. But even before the car stopped, the front door on the passenger side flew open and Earl Durand ran off into the darkness. For a second Bennion had him in the flashlight beam, then he was gone, moving silently through the dark stones and brambles leading up and over the mountain.

When you dress game you get awful messy. Blood and hair are always all over a person who's cleaned game or handled the carcass. Just by looking us boys over with his flashlight, Bennion knew he had his poachers. You don't have to search a car to see if there's game inside. It's easy to tell when someone's bagged an elk or deer. You can spot hair all over his clothes. When you come in at night after a day's hunting, no one has to ask if you were successful. The hair and blood—that's the telltale thing. Tom and I were a mess even though we had rubbed bunches of grass all over us to get it off back where we had killed the elk. Bennion asked, "Where's the meat?" That's all there was to it. He had us nailed. He walked to the back of the car and opened the trunk. Then he came back and talked to Dad.

"We had the pleasure of meeting this afternoon." He was being sarcastic. "But you're a long way from Powell. I didn't get your name, neighbor. What is it?"

"Knopp. Gus Knopp."

Bennion said, "Mr. Knopp, follow me to the courthouse and don't try anything funny."

As we drove off I said, "I think that guy is an eager beaver." Dad said, "That's enough from you. You dang kids got me into this trouble, now keep your smart-aleck comments to yourself."

Nobody said a word the rest of the way to the courthouse. As we drove toward town, I worried. Earl had had a few scrapes with the law, I knew. And now people were going to think we were mixed up with him, which we were. This was the worst thing Tom or I had ever done. All our earlier mischief was kids' play by comparison.

What was Dad thinking? What would my stepmother say when she heard? Tom and me had gone deep enough into trouble, but as it turned out, Earl was just getting started.

I knew my father was ashamed and angry all at the same time. As soon as we got out of the car, the two game wardens took us into the jail. Deputy sheriff Noah Riley inked our fingers and took our prints.

Bennion wrote up the charges against us. Then we went into the courtroom where we waited while the judge finished his dinner at home. Before he came down, he called and talked to the game wardens, but we couldn't hear what they said even though we were in the same room. In the middle of the trouble, Tom decided to get a chip on his shoulder and said to the game warden, real smart, "I'm hungry. I need some food. I haven't eaten since lunch."

"This ain't a restaurant, kid. The prisoners already had supper. Next meal is breakfast," Bennion said sarcastically.

Then King chimed in. "What would you like to order? Mrs. Riley makes good eggs and sausage. Stick around. You'll have a plenty big appetite by breakfast time."

They were rubbing it in.

When justice of the peace and judge Walter Owens arrived, he had us brought into the courtroom. The judge read out the charges against my father of being an accomplice to poaching elk. Then he asked, "How do you plead, Mr. Knopp?"

"Guilty, sir," answered my father.

"I sentence you to sixty days in the county jail and a one hundred dollar fine."

It was over that quick.

There was a look of pain on Dad's face. "Judge, I don't have one hundred dollars to pay, and sixty days in jail when planting is about to start..." His voice trailed off. Dad was crushed. I thought he was going to cry.

Then the judge called Dad up to the bench and talked to him in private. The judge wanted to find out what had happened. When they finished, the judge said out loud, "I'm sorry, Mr. Knopp, but you know poaching is illegal." Then he said, "I don't want your car around here for two months. Can your son drive?"

Dad said, "Yes." The state of Wyoming didn't require driver's licenses at the time.

The judge sure didn't want two young kids taking up space in the jail and eating like horses at the taxpayers' expense. Instead, he gave Tom and me a tongue-lashing that was supposed to raise welts on our tender souls. "And you two. Mr. Knopp tells me you're friends of this Durand character. He's no good and he's turnin' you to no good. You talked your father into this. Your father is an upstanding citizen. Look what you've gotten him into." He was right.

The judge asked, "Who'll tend the livestock while he's in jail? The son he has to blame for his misfortune? You two boys deserve the licking of your lives, no matter how old you are." He paused and glowered.

Then he said, "Promise good behavior from now on. Go on. Let me hear it."

The judge really had no choice about locking up my father, though Tom and I could tell he didn't want to do it. But now Tom, like a fool, showed off and acted like he was a tough guy in front of the judge.

"I ain't promising nothing," Tom growled. "When you let me go, I'm going back out to the mountain, find Earl, and stay with him." Tom wouldn't let well enough alone.

I couldn't stand it. Here was this kind old Judge Owens giving us a break and Tom was trying to queer it, make himself out to be a badman. I said, "Your honor, Tom is only speaking for himself. I am sorry for what I did. I have nothing to do with what Spint is saying." Tom turned to me and spat, "Chicken!"

"Quit pretending to be an outlaw," I said. "You have no idea where Earl is. He could be anywhere within forty miles of the mountain."

"The hell with you, then."

The judge said, "I have had just about enough. One more word from you, Spint, and I'll sentence you for poaching and contempt of court. Now you set yourself down this instant."

I wasn't an angel, but I wasn't a fool either. Here was Tom acting like a tough guy and trying to drag me along with him. Who needs a friend like that?

Then the judge said, "The court orders the two of you to tend the livestock until Mr. Knopp has served his sentence. Ronnie, your stepmother will have to arrange with the neighbors to have the fields worked and seeded." Then he dismissed us. "Go wait in the jail. Spint, does your family have a phone?" Tom nodded. The judge told the bailiff, "Call Mr. Spint and have him come pick his son up."

Then he turned to me and said, "You drive your father's car home tonight and only go where your stepmother sends you. I don't want you taking your friend home. Besides, I need to talk to Spint's father." Then he said, "And I don't want you joy riding around while your father's in jail." The judge turned to the bailiff and said, "Lock the prisoner up. He starts serving his sentence now."

Dad always paid his bills on time, never disobeyed a law, never committed a crime. People were like that then. He was a member of the Grange and we went to church every Sunday. I knew I'd never hear the end of this. You'd think we had killed somebody to see how solemn they treated us. There'd be no living it down, ever.

My father called my stepmother and told her what had happened. She got a ride to Cody with Mr. Spint. I wasn't looking forward to facing her. You know that expression "livid with rage"? When she came through the door and caught sight of me, that's just what she turned. I drove her home. It was another quiet ride, then a rough evening at home. My stepmother had a lot to say about me and Earl. "The whole plan was ignorant and foolish! Now your father is paying for listening to you. Now what will people think of us? How will we ever be able to hold our heads up in church?" She harangued me all evening. Right then I decided to spend the next night at the Spint house. As bad as I felt about Tom, I felt that much worse about my stepmother.

I CALL EVERYTHING UP TO this point "the beginning" because what Earl did the next morning changed the whole complexion of events. Poaching is illegal, but here in Wyoming, killing a beef cow is *against the law!* Every Wyomingite knows from the cradle on up, whatever else you may do wrong, you never kill a cow unless it's wearing your brand. Wildlife belongs to the state, but cattle are someone's personal property, their way to make a living, so in Wyoming killing a beef cow isn't just a felony, it's a crime against civilization!

But the next morning, kill a beef is just what Earl did.

I wasn't there, but from what everybody says, this is the way it happened.

The homestead closest to that tunnel where we'd been nabbed was the Yeates ranch, right up at the head of Shoshone Canyon. Long before sunup, rancher Johnny Yeates was lying in bed half awake when he heard rifle shots. His two ranch hands in the bunkhouse heard them, too. Leonard Morris asked, "Did you hear anything?" The other ranch hand, Tex Kennedy, answered, "Rifle shots. Better go see."

They threw their clothes on and rushed outside. Mr. Yeates was already coming toward the bunkhouse. "I heard gunfire. Saddle up and let's find out what's going on. Bring your rifles."

The three of them rode out to the range, and soon Morris found a wounded cow. Then Kennedy called over, "Here's a dead calf." As they dismounted Mr. Yeates said, "I'll be damned! Whoever killed this calf carved a chunk of tenderloin right out of it."

"There must be some lunatic running loose," said Kennedy.

Yeates said, "Throw the calf over your horse's back. Bring it in and butcher it. Then get the cow to the corral. Maybe we can save it."

They mounted up and headed back to the ranch house. "I'll see the son of a bitch in jail!" Yeates cursed, steaming mad. "Who in this day and age would kill a beef in the state of Wyoming?" asked Morris as they trotted along.

When they got back to the ranch, Yeates called the sheriff's office and spoke to Noah Riley. "Some son of a bitch killed one of my calves and wounded a cow. The damnedest thing is, he cut a chunk of tenderloin out of that little heifer."

As I said, Earl did eat raw meat. I tried it, but I still eat my steak medium, not rare. He always carried parched corn and raisins, mixed, and ate dried venison for his lunch. That wasn't at all bad, but I leave raw meat alone. Earl had a taste for it.

"Durand done it," said Riley.

"Who?"

"Earl Durand."

"How do you know?" asked the rancher. "And who the hell is Earl Durand?"

"Just wait and see. Durand is a local smalltime outlaw. He likes to vandalize cabins and steal whatever he wants. He poached some elk yesterday and got away from the wardens. We'll catch the SOB and take him out of circulation for a good long spell, if you'll press charges. Who you have out there I can deputize?"

"Tex Kennedy and Leonard Morris."

"Good. I'll be there as quick as I can. I'll bring some game wardens, too."

Mr. Yeates said, "We'll be waiting for you."

SEVERAL INCHES OF WET snow had fallen during the night and covered the North Fork highway. The men had to drive slow, but they were in no particular hurry. Earl couldn't be too far away. Snow covered everything except the faces of the gray rocks—camouflage for Earl on a day with a sky cloudy with storm and storm winds blowing.

The posse started searching right where Earl had jumped from the car the night before. Bennion said, "I've got a feeling that he's up here again." The men traipsed around for a couple of minutes, then Bennion spotted tracks. "I'll be damned. Just like I said, he's up there." They climbed quickly. King took out his binoculars, looked around and discovered Durand half a mile up on Rattlesnake Mountain. He was right behind a boulder perched on a steep slope in the blind canyon. It was near the place he had taken me that night the previous fall, the place where we stayed up all night to watch the sky wheel overhead. Why he picked that spot now I'll never know. Boyd Bennion signaled to the men to take cover and said in a loud whisper, "Nowhere he can go. He's dangerous as a wildcat."

Earl had his rifle ready.

Morris was bringing up the rear. Seeing the men up ahead of him drop, he knew to stay back out of sight. He could tell where Durand was by where the others were looking. Morris circled back and down, then crept around up above Earl. He moved quickly and quietly. The posse could tell that Durand hadn't spotted Morris. When Morris got within range, he shouted out, "We got you covered, Durand! Drop your gun and put your hands up!" Earl spun toward Morris, who fired over his head. Durand dropped his rifle, put up his hands and surrendered. It was over that quick. Morris brought Earl in at gunpoint. Tex Kennedy went back after Earl's rifle.

"Good job," Riley said. He turned to Durand and said with a scowl, "You're under arrest, you damned fool. Poaching and killing a beef cow! What the hell's the matter with you? Who the hell you think you are, mister mountain man? It'll be a cold day in hell before you see a mountain again. You're plumb loco as far as I'm concerned." He turned back to Morris and told him, "Slap handcuffs on him and march him down off to jail. Take what's left of the chunk of beef hanging from the cord around his neck. We'll hold it for the judge as evidence."

They cuffed Earl's hands behind his back. It was hard for him to keep his balance as he made his way down the mountain's treacherous slope.

Before he killed that calf, Earl could have just marched into town and turned himself in to the deputy sheriff. He would have got some extra time and maybe a little more fine for resisting arrest, but turning himself in would have helped a lot. And that would have been it. Or he could have hiked thirty or forty miles by morning in any direction he pleased. Earl had what he called "nests" and "forts" all over the countryside, from Jackson Hole at the southern tip of the Tetons to as far north as the Beartooths and all through the crescent of the Big Horns. But Earl just stayed put, not more than a couple hundred yards from where he had jumped out of the car. There was no figuring out what he was thinking, what he had in mind. Something was out of whack.

The next afternoon I drove my stepmother back to Cody to visit my dad. Before we went into the jail, she said, "Now you apologize to your father for all the trouble you made and beg his forgiveness."

"Aw, nuts," I protested.

Shaking her finger, she said, "Young man, you do as I say. You deserve a thorough thrashing, you torment and trouble, and when your father gets home I hope he gives you one."

She was right. I at least owed him an apology.

When I saw him in jail I said, "I'm sorry, Dad. I really am. I wish we'd never gone out after them elk."

Dad was glum and angry the whole time of our visit. I left Dad and my stepmother fuming and sputtering together, making plans about caring for the livestock, plowing the fields, getting the crops planted. Meanwhile Earl was pacing around in his cell like a bear at the zoo. I wandered off to talk to him. He came over to the bars and stood there. At first I couldn't think of anything to say. So I asked a dumb question just to be talking, "Where did you spend the night? I'm sure you got out of the wind."

"I hunted up a cave up on Cedar Mountain, pulled in a bunch of dead grass and slept. I woke up hungry. We didn't eat yesterday so I went down and got myself some beef."

"Beef? Where'd you get beef?"

Then he said, "I killed a calf and cut out its tenderloin."

This was the first I heard about his killing a calf. What had Earl been thinking? His mind must have snapped. And why had Earl stayed right there, near the same place where he had jumped from the car? That was a spot as bad as you could pick unless you wanted no way out for yourself. I'd read dozens of stories in Earl's Western magazines, dozens, where a guy on the "hoot-owl trail," a night rider, trapped himself in a canyon. You might think that where he was caught proves he wasn't thinking right. But something was wrong even before that. By the time he killed that calf, crazy thinking had replaced the clear thoughts of the mountain man.

I couldn't even imagine that my friend kill a calf. I knew that Earl was in deep trouble now.

"Earl, you knew better than to kill a calf. Poaching's one thing and this is another. What were you thinking?"

Earl sat down on the iron bed and just stared at the wall. He wasn't even listening. "They want to take away my freedom," he said. Then he was quiet again. Earl was talking strange. I was worried. He was thinking real hard and not listening. Then I asked, just wanting to make conversation, "How did they catch you?"

Earl said, "All I remember is I was I looking down the barrel of a pistol and it seemed big enough to turn a flock of sheep in." Suddenly he was angry and agitated. "I'm going to be charged with killing that calf. They're gonna take away my freedom!" he said again. Earl quieted down, put his head in his hands, and just sat there. After a while he looked up at me like he was surprised to see me. Then he motioned for me to come closer and whispered, "Go to my tent. Collect all of my guns and cache them at your place. Hold them for me till I get out of jail." I thought he meant until after he'd served the six-month sentence he'd been handed, at least, not to mention the time he might spend in the state penitentiary. Earl didn't say a word about planning to escape.

"I can't eat this jail food. I need something more raw," said Earl. He fished a dollar out of his pocket and handed it to me. "Run out and get me a pound of wieners."

I crossed the street to the grocery store, bought the wieners, ran right back to the jail, and gave them to Earl. While Durand was gobbling down his wieners Riley came in. He looked at Durand eating and muttered, "No buns, no mustard, no relish, no kraut, no nothing but cold wieners." He walked away, shaking his head in disgust.

Then my stepmother and I left for home.

That was the last time I ever saw Earl Durand.

WHEN MY STEPMOTHER AND I got home I did my chores, then snuck out, ran over to the Durand place, and crept into Earl's tent. I wrapped his best guns in a canvas tarp, carried them home, climbed to the back of the hayloft, dug a hole in the hay, and buried them there.

The next evening Earl broke jail, taking Noah Riley along with him. Earl made Riley drive him to our farm first—but nobody was home. "Honk the horn," he told him, and Riley did. When they drove in the yard, only the porch light was on. Earl had come by planning to get his guns. He must have wondered where I was. But I hadn't been expecting him so soon.

My mother had gone to visit my father in jail. A neighbor had given her a ride, and she had arranged for me to have dinner with the Spints.

Tom and I were eating chicken noodle soup, grilled cheese sandwiches, and green tomato relish Tom's mother had pickled that fall. The radio was on, but we weren't paying it much attention. Tom was saying, "Pass me the relish, will ya?" when a voice broke in.

"We interrupt this program for an important bulletin. The sheriff's office of Park Count…"

"Shush!" I hissed at Tom.

"... *reports the escape of...* "

"And another sandwich," Tom said.

"...*from the county jail in Cody.*"

"Someone broke jail in Cody!" I said.

"How do you know?"

"Dammit, that's why I wanted you to be quiet. It came over the radio."

"Who was it?"

"I couldn't hear."

Since my dad and Earl were in jail, I wanted to know what had happened. Tom said, "I suspicion it must be Earl."

"Let's ride into town and ask at the sheriff's office."

We jumped in his father's old Model T and drove to the deputy sheriff's office in Powell. Old Mr. Baker and Chuck Lewis were inside strapping on their six-shooters and grabbing their guns. The sheriff's office in Cody must have called them for help. I asked, "Who broke jail?"

Lewis said, "Out of the way, you kids."

"I'm Ronnie Knopp and my father and my friend are in jail there. Who broke out?"

Baker moved toward the door. "We've got work to do."

"But it's my dad!"

"Get the hell out of our way," said Lewis.

They chased us out of the office, came out behind us, then took off in their car. It was new and fast and we were in an old Model T. Tom drove and we followed. Sure enough, they headed for the Durand place, pulling farther ahead of us all the time. Finally we lost sight of them. It was just dark. When we got within about two hundred yards of the Durands' driveway, we saw a couple flashes of gunfire in the yard. Us young fools kept right on. We drove in the yard and come within a foot of driving over Baker's head. He was lying in the driveway. When we spotted him, I shouted, "Holy cow! He's dead!" Spint put that Model T in reverse, and did we get the hell out of there. We were scared to death. We knew Earl had broken out of jail. We had suspicioned it, but now we knew for sure. And now we knew he had killed a poor old deputy. Later I learned that he'd killed both deputies from Powell—Chuck Lewis and old Mr. Baker—and he'd shot Noah Riley in the leg. As bad as things had been before, they were a hell of a lot worse now.

TOM STARTED ACTING neighborly. Every day he came over to help me with my chores after he finished his. It worked out good for me because I sure needed the help. I had more on my hands than I could handle—my own chores on top of Dad's work. Even so, we had a little time to play around. One afternoon a few days after Earl escaped from jail, we drove to the hardware store in Powell. I had trapped and skinned out a couple dozen muskrat and wanted to trade the pelts for a new skinning knife that I had had my eye on for quite a while. After I bought it, I had enough left over to buy a couple boxes of rifle shells.

The next day after school, Tom and I were feeding the animals when a car drove into the yard. I could see three men, two in front and one in back. The driver rolled down his window and I recognized Jimmy Dutton. He owned a gas and repair station in Ralston. But he didn't know me. He asked, real friendly, "Which one of you boys is Ronnie Knopp?"

"I am."

"Son, your dad wants to see you. Get in and come along with us."

"I'll be back tonight, won't I?"

"Sure, kid." He spoke loud. I guess they were afraid Earl might be hiding at our place. They didn't want to do anything to arouse his suspicions. Since Earl had killed two lawmen, the possemen knew he'd be willing to kill them, too.

I turned to Tom. "Can you finish up the chores for me?"

"Yeah, I guess so."

Tucked away in the back seat where I couldn't see his face was Boyd Bennion, the game warden who had arrested us.

The front door on the passenger side opened and Vern Spencer, a local hunting guide and outfitter, got out. I knew him, too. He opened the back door and motioned for me to get in. Then he slammed the front door and got in next to me. As soon as he closed the door, Spencer grabbed me and slapped handcuffs on me. I shouted, "You stinkin' liars!" and we tussled as I tried to get loose. The men were all deputized—deputy sheriffs.

Even though it was March and pretty cold, they rolled down three of the windows and stuck their guns out, ready to shoot if they saw Earl. Bennion said to Jimmy Dutton, "Hotfoot it out of here! Durand might be watching us bundle his kid off." Changing his tune, he said to me, "Kid, you're arrested as being Durand's accomplice. You bought a knife and ammunition for him." His voice rose. "Where is he? For all I know Earl is holed up somewhere here with his gun leveled at us right now. But you know where he is, don't you, kid?"

"I don't know what you're talking about! I sold some muskrat skins and bought hunting supplies."

"Bullshit!" Bennion said. "Where is Durand? Is he hiding at your place? Where is he?"

The guy who put the handcuffs on me added his two cents' worth. "He's got 'criminal' written all over his face," said Spencer. "He learned from Earl Durand."

Dutton said, "Keep your eyes peeled! Durand might try to waylay us."

Bennion said, "He could just that easy pop up in the middle of the road over the hill."

They were pretty nervous. Only one was a regular law officer. The rest were cowboys and hunting guides who had been deputized.

It turns out Spint had snuck off after our visit to the hardware store and called the police. He pretended to be a store employee and tipped them off that I had bought the knife and ammo. He also told the police I had said I was a friend of Durand's and was buying all the stuff for Earl. Tom Spint was like poison. You couldn't tell by looking at him that he was deadly—just like a piece of meat sprinkled with arsenic. I thought to myself, that damned snitch. He was a snake, a stinking skunk. Like a sidewinder, one minute he was wanting to run off and be an outlaw with Earl, and the next he was snitching and lying to the police while pretending he was my friend.

They drove me to the little jail in Powell where Noah Riley was waiting for me. Guess they didn't want me in the Cody jail where my dad was. Noah Riley's head was completely bandaged. He had a gash in his head and a mild concussion from the blow Earl had dealt him. He looked terrible, like he'd had the whipping of his life. By then he'd already got the nickname "Milk Bottle" for what Earl had hit him with. Some kid from school had gone with his father to the Ames department store. He overheard a customer joke about the name with a clerk and the name traveled all over school like wildfire. I was feeling a little too brassy when I saw Riley there and muttered "Milk Bottle Riley" loud enough for all the men to hear.

I don't know if Riley had heard the name before or not, but he was mean to begin with. "Tell me where Earl is, or I'll see you hang!" He threatened the holy hell out of me. "I'll get answers!" he said.

Then Riley ordered Spencer, "Guard the door!" and barked to Jimmy Dutton, "Shackle his legs," tossing over a set of shackles. Riley kept asking me about Earl, but I just kept my mouth shut. I didn't know where Earl was; not a soul knew where he was. Then Riley growled, "Book the little bastard! We already got his prints." Then he stormed out of the jail.

From the Powell jail they hustled me to Basin where I got free room and board in the county jail. I was by myself. I sat there until the day Earl died. Nobody visited me. Nobody would tell me what was happening. I asked for the newspaper, but the guards would only let me have the sports and comics. They wouldn't talk to me about Earl.

I remembered a story we read in school called "The Man Without a Country." Every school kid knows it: it's about a man who said he never wanted to hear the name of the United States again, so he was condemned to spend the rest of his life on ships. The sailors were forbidden to speak with him about the country or show him any newspapers or books that mentioned the United States. The idea is, the man regretted what he said and suffered for it all his life. I felt like that man, only I couldn't understand why they wouldn't tell me about my friend. They were punishing me, but I didn't make a fuss over it. I didn't want to let them know it hurt me and I was lonely. I didn't know a thing about what Earl had done since I saw him in jail.

A few days later, after Earl was dead, the damned stinkers brought me from Basin and stuck me in the Cody jail for a couple more days before they let me go. I was never charged with anything. I never saw a judge. I was never tried. I just sat there with nothing to do, then they let me go. Maybe the law thought I would help Earl. I would have given him his guns. They were his property. I would have given him food. But there was nothing else I could do. I never saw my friend again after I visited him in jail. The law didn't give me a chance.

After I was hauled off, Tom quit coming to do the chores, just quit cold, the rat. My father was still in jail. My stepmother had to call up my brother, Ed, over in Gillette for help. He had only been on his job a few months. His boss wouldn't give him time off, so he had to quit and come back home to run the farm.

While I was in jail, Tom swiped all Earl's guns that I had hidden, the old stinker. I don't know how he found out about my hiding them, but somehow he did. Maybe he had visited Earl in jail and Earl told him. When I got home they were gone.

I went back to school the next day. I was treated as a kind of hero. Then I ran into Spint. I was coming out of shop class and he was coming in. There was a bunch of boys around. We were changing classes. Spint started mouthing off, calling me a jailbird. I shot back real quick, "And you're a damned snitch, a liar, and a thief!" The boys standing around pricked up their ears when they heard what we said. I said, "You damned louse! You stole Earl's guns." A couple of the boys egged us on to fight. I said, "I have more ownership over them than you do. Earl gave them to me to take care of, and that's just what I aim to do. You stole 'em. Now give 'em back to me!"

Tom backed off and said, "I dropped them all off the river bridge at Willwood."

"You're a stinking liar. I know you wouldn't throw good guns in the river. What did you do with them?" I had the liar nailed. Spint came at me with a roundhouse punch and missed by a mile. I stormed up on him and laced into him. In one good swipe, I had him sprawled on his back. Then he got up and come on like fury. We slugged it out, kicking, twisting arms, a real rip-roarer. It wasn't a fight to the finish, but it sure was bloody. This bum betrayed Earl, and he betrayed me. He was only out for himself.

The shop teacher came out and pulled us apart. We were both sent to the principal. Tom was suspended for a week and I was expelled from school. The principal said I couldn't return till next year. That was the end of it. There was nothing else I could do. Later on I found out Spint picked out a gun or two for himself, sold the rest, and pocketed the money. It was just like I thought.

Now my stepmother could barely stand the sight of me. I could almost see her hackles raise up every time we ran into each other. She always had some unpleasant remark to make. It was worse than before.

My father was let out of jail after serving thirty days. I think the judge took pity on him and let him out early. But even after my dad got home and things calmed down, my folks were bitter with me. We argued and fought. I couldn't blame them, but I couldn't stand it either. I felt like I was no longer welcome in the family. I wanted out, so just like Earl used to do, I left. But I wasn't going off to be a mountain man. I wasn't loading up a pack with grub and clothes and ammunition. I was leaving home, leaving for good. I never expected to leave my father high and dry, but here I was giving up the farm. I'd have made a darn good farmer, too. I was angry and sad at the same time.

I went west to Oregon, found work fishing and mining. When the war broke out I enlisted. It wasn't till I was overseas that I started writing to my family and they started writing back to me.

When we went hunting that day I never would have guessed that things would turn out the way they did. It was a sickening hell of a mess.

FOR YEARS PEOPLE HAVE been at this story with their "ifs"—if Frank Blackburn had been here in Cody instead of off at the World's Fair in San Francisco, if Noah Riley had taken his pistol out of its holster before he went into Earl's cell the way he was supposed to, if Chuck Lewis and Baker had done what Earl's father told them to do when they got out of their car, if we had poached on land where there was no cabin… Folks think of "ifs" as though they could prevent something from happening. But the way I see it, "ifs" just as much cause events as prevent them. You could even say everything fell into place perfectly, everybody in the right place at the right time. Look at it this way: if only my father had bought land on a different section, I never would have become close friends with Earl. What I mean is, the smallest change in the sequence of events, no matter how remotely connected, would have caused the whole thing to turn out completely different. Did Earl teach me this? Hell, no. But in a way he did. Not just Earl, but the way the whole thing unfolded.

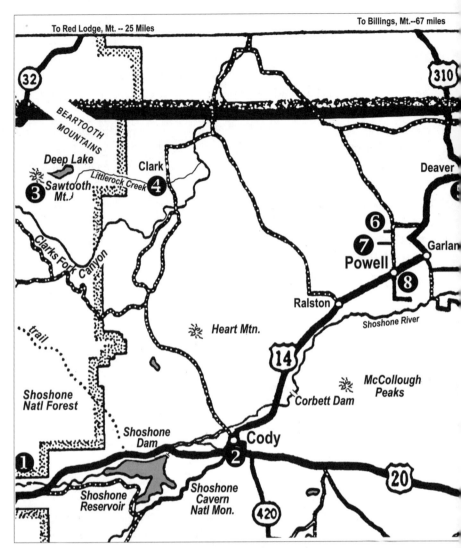

1. Vicinity where Durand and friends poached the elk
2. Location of Park County Jail in Cody where Durand was held
3. Area where Durand made a stand against the posse
4. Posse headquarters at a ranch
5. Location where Durand picked up ammunition
6. The farm owned by Durand's parents
7. Where Durand released his passengers before going to Powell
8. Location of bank robbery in downtown Powell

THE JAILBREAK &
FIRST MURDERS

About 5 o'clock Thursday evening Undersheriff Noah
Riley, upon entering his jail cell, was struck over the
head a stunning blow by Durand, who used a milk
bottle as a weapon. Riley was bereft of his shooting arms.

Powell Tribune, March 16

Durand, who at 26 has become almost a legendary figure
because of his skill in all the mountain crafts and his penchant
for eating raw meat and living as far removed as possible
from civilization, shot and killed Undersheriff D.M. Baker
and Town Marshall Chuck Lewis of Powell last Thursday night.

Denver Post, March 25

MILWARD L. SIMPSON

CODY LAWYER,
LATER GOVERNOR AND SENATOR

IT WAS A SHAME SHERIFF Frank Blackburn was out of town. I wouldn't be surprised to discover that somehow Earl knew the sheriff was away, but that had nothing to do with what Earl did. It was just a coincidence.

For some time Frank's friends had encouraged him to take his wife, Jenny, on a vacation, but the farthest he would go was Denver. The sheriff was always on the job. He was one of the last of the old-time sheriffs. He took his profession seriously. The Park County Sheriff's Department had a right to be proud. The sheriff prevented crime. Everyone knew that if you disobeyed the law in Park County, justice would be done. That's how it was, though to tell the truth, the community was as straight arrow as its sheriff. No "bad element" ever gained a foothold here, not that they didn't try. Tourists visited Cody in the summer, so we had a lot of people pass through, the kind grifters and pickpockets prey on. But the word was out: this is a town where the dishonest are ordered out of town before sunset or land in jail. We didn't believe in a jail too comfortable either.

The sheriff was busy during Prohibition. Most people think about the South when you talk about bootlegging. But there was a lot of bootlegging all through the mountains hereabouts. When Frank got wind of a still, he'd pursue it day and night till he found still and bootlegger, then nailed shut the arrest and conviction. He was just that way. Of course there is always a certain amount of nuisance crime around. As one of the town's few lawyers, I handled enough of the cases, but it never amounted to much—an occasional breaking and entering up in a mountain camp, speeding tickets, a stolen gun, drunk and disorderly, poachings like Durand's, misdemeanors of one sort or another. When Earl Durand was arrested no one was too surprised.

Earl's arrest was the first step in the biggest crime spree this neck of the woods ever saw. That was surprising. As bad as Kid Curry, Butch Cassidy, and the Sundance Kid were, and as long as they and their cohorts over in the Hole in the Wall were at large, none of them killed as many innocent men in such a short time as Earl Durand. He left wounds in our community that were a long time in healing. Brokenhearted parents—including his own, and the families and friends of the dead men remember him with pain and anger. The lives of everyone touched by the events underwent some change, some shift, and usually for the worse.

Frank Blackburn was considerably older than me. I knew him since I was a kid. I attended his wedding when I was fourteen. My mother, Maggie, was a witness—along with Colonel Cody's sister. I found out where the couple was going to spend the night and organized the charivari. The rams and stags who came to the wedding brought kettles, pans, washboards, kazoos, harmonicas, slide whistles, jew's harps and such. We serenaded the bride and groom on their marriage night. In the middle of our performance, Frank opened the window and tossed out an envelope. We expected it to be the customary bribe to shut up the cat-howling and raucous noise. But instead there was a message on a piece of lady's scented notepaper:

> "Never was heard such a noise, row, hubbub, babel, shindy, hullabaloo, stramash, charivari and total contempt of dignity and order." Kingsley, *The Water-Babies*

Frank was an educated man. His quoting from the children's book was a good shot back, a good retort.

The sheriff couldn't remember when he had last taken an honest-to-goodness vacation. So when a writ came through from the San Francisco Police Department to extradite a character, the sheriff agreed to take Mrs. Blackburn and his son, Frank Junior, along to San Francisco. They planned to take in the World's Fair on Treasure

Island. All along the sheriff was reluctant, but finally the family drove off.

His friends never heard the end of it, as if we had invited Durand to poach and break jail since we knew the sheriff was away. I could tell that this would be Frank's last vacation. He'd been proved right— a sheriff should never take a vacation. We could never talk him into another one, couldn't persuade him that he needed to get away with his family once in a while so they could renew old acquaintances.

RIGHT OFF YOU COULD TELL there was going to be serious trouble. Not only had Durand escaped arrest and been involved in some odd doings—he had a piece of chawed tenderloin on a string around his neck—but he acted up pretty badly in the Cody jail and in court. I've talked to most of the men involved and, though lots of stories circulated, I think this is what happened next. After Judge Walter Owens sentenced poor Mr. Knopp, the judge called game warden Bennion in to confer with him. "What are your plans for catching this Durand fella?"

"No point hunting him in the dark," Bennion answered. "But it's really up to the sheriff and his people what they want to do."

The judge said, "The sheriff is in California extraditing a prisoner and taking a family vacation. Noah Riley is in charge. He's new and I hear he's pretty bull-headed, likes to take matters into his own hands, so to speak. He'll need all the advice he can get. I'll call him and let him know what he needs to do. I'll have him get hold of you this evening. The two of you make your plans. Poachers are a pain in the neck. I hope this one doesn't give you too much trouble."

"He already has," Bennion said.

When the men reached the jail, Deputy Riley locked Durand's gun and hunting knife in the sheriff's gun cabinet and told game warden Dwight King, "Put your gun on 'im. I'm gonna take his fingerprints." Riley unlocked Durand's handcuffs. He asked Earl, "You been fingerprinted before? We'll find out quick enough." He took two sets of fingerprints and gave one set to King. "Send these off to the FBI. This set's for us." He turned to Durand again. "We're gonna check you out. I've heard about you before. Nobody ever wanted to file charges against you. I heard they took care of you in their own way. You've stepped over the line before around here. But this time you went way the hell over. And we got you!"

Durand asked, "What's all the fuss about? All I wanted was a little meat. I live in the mountains and have to get my food the best way I can. I don't believe in those laws that say a man can't shoot wild animals when he needs to eat."

"From what I hear you don't respect property rights either. But this ain't about your gun-thieving and such. You killed someone's heifer!"

Even as he was being locked in the jail cell, Durand was still mumbling and complaining. "I don't see why I gotta go to jail. All I wanted was a little elk meat."

As he was locking the door, Riley said, "Wait till the judge hauls you out and asks how you plead on killing Johnny Yeates's calf. You could get twenty years in the state pen. You'll forget what the mountains look like before you get out of Rawlins, you damned fool!"

Glowering, Earl stood close to the cell door, squeezing the bars as Riley taunted him.

Later that day Earl was brought before the county court judge. "Mr. Durand, I am the same judge who tried Mr. Knopp's case and sentenced him to sixty days in jail and a one hundred-dollar fine," Owens told him. The he turned and said, "Bailiff, read out the charge."

"In the case of Park County versus Earl Durand in the matter of poaching elk out of season and resisting arrest."

Owens asked, "Mr. Durand, how do you plead?"

Earl complained, "I didn't do anything wrong. What's wrong with getting a little meat when a family needs it?"

"Excuse me, Mr. Durand. Guilty or not guilty?"

"I ain't guilty! I live by what I can shoot."

The judge heard the testimony of the two game wardens and Noah Riley. Then he asked, "Mr. Durand, do you have any witnesses, or is there anything you want to say in your own defense?" Earl started in again on his points. This happens a lot with cowboys and mountain men. They don't understand court proceedings and there's no reason they should. Judge Owens let him go on for a while, then said, "Mr. Durand, face the bench." Then he lowered the boom. "Because of your attempted escape from the officers, Earl

Durand, to teach you to have some respect for the law, you are sentenced to pay a fine of a hundred dollars and to serve six months in the county jail."

Durand's face clouded over. You could almost read his thoughts: "They won't keep me in jail long!"

Earl spent the night in jail. The next morning his parents, Walter and Effie Durand, a highly respected and honest farm couple, came to Cody hoping to negotiate with the county officials. Meeting with county attorney Oliver Steadman at his office, the sad, careworn couple asked if they could do anything to get their son out of jail.

Steadman said, "No, and it looks like Earl is going to be charged with killing Johnny Yeates's heifer. If Earl is found guilty, he'll serve his sentence at the state penitentiary in Rawlins. It remains to be seen if Yeates will prosecute. You might want to talk to him."

Mr. Durand turned to his wife and said, "Maybe we can pay for the heifer as restitution. I'm sure the rancher will be reasonable. Earl can work it off." They didn't stay more than a minute or two. They said what they had to say, left Steadman's office, and went to the jail to visit their son. They told him what the attorney had said. When they left the jail, they had no idea that Earl would break out.

AND THAT WAS HOW MATTERS stood until five o'clock on the evening of the sixteenth, when Noah Riley brought dinner to the prisoners. Riley put the tray down on a table near Earl's cell door and put the key in the lock. Ordinarily he unlocked the door, gave it a slight push, then stepped back to survey the cell's interior before going in. But this time, as soon as he turned the key in the lock, the door flew open and Durand leaped out. Startled, Riley quickly stepped back and tried to pull his gun from its holster. He should have taken it off and left it in the office. You don't carry a pistol into a jail cell. Durand grabbed the thick pint milk bottle from the tray and brought it down with a crashing blow on the deputy's head, opening a gash in Riley's scalp. Dazed and suffering from scalding pain, Riley could make only a feeble effort to hold Durand off. Sprawled on the broken glass and milk and food mixed with his own blood, Riley stared up at Durand who was pointing the gun at him.

Earl said, "Get up on your feet! I'm getting out of here and you're coming with me!" Much bigger and more powerful than Riley, the young man forced him to march to the sheriff's locked gun cabinet. Wiping blood from the officer's face, Earl pointed to the sheriff's high-powered automatic rifle. He said, "Hand me my rifle and knife and give me that rifle and clip, too." Riley was so weak from the blow that he couldn't do what Earl told him to. Durand grabbed Riley's keys and asked, "Which one is it?" The deputy pointed out the key. Earl grabbed the rifle and the one clip of shells he could see.

"Get me more shells," he ordered.

"There aren't any more."

"You're lying. How could the sheriff have a rifle and no shells? I ain't stupid."

"I don't know where he keeps them. He hides them away in case of something like this happening. He doesn't want to send the likes of you off with a gol-dang arsenal."

"Well, don't worry. I've got plenty more shells where we're going. Get out to your car." Earl couldn't find his knife, so they left without it.

Riley stumbled ahead. "You drive," Earl said, and Riley dragged himself into his own car on the driver's side. Blood pouring over his face, he remained conscious only by sheer willpower.

"We're going out to my dad's place. Do as I say and you'll be okay, but don't try anything funny. Keep your hands on the wheel," Durand ordered. "I'll keep the blood off so you can see." He mopped Riley's face with his bandanna. "If any trouble starts, you're my hostage, damn you. You ain't gonna put me in jail again."

There was really no telling what Durand had in mind, beyond escaping. "You don't want to go through with this, Earl," Riley managed to say. "If you keep up, you're gonna get into real trouble."

"Shut up and drive," Durand said. "I couldn't stand it in that hole anymore. The air's bad."

But as the car left Cody, traveling down Sheridan Avenue toward Powell, high school bandmaster Merle Prugh passed them heading the opposite direction on his way home. He was an acquaintance of Riley's. Noticing blood on Riley's face, he made a U-turn and followed. Riley saw Prugh and hoped he could help, but Earl noticed the car catching up too, and ordered Riley to slow down.

As Prugh's car drew closer, Durand motioned with Riley's six-shooter for him to turn back. At first hesitating, Prugh finally obeyed Durand's gestures, turned, and rushed to Oliver Steadman's house to spread the alarm.

As he drove toward Powell, Riley was nearly overcome by weakness. He carried a tear-gas gun in his pocket and tried to reach it. But each time he moved his hand, it went against his bidding and raised itself to his wound. And each time, Durand barked, "Keep your hands on that wheel!" jabbing Riley's side with the deputy's own six-shooter.

After a while Durand spoke up about himself. "They arrested me in Suaguache, Colorado, when I was twenty. I avoided traveled roads to see if I could make it to New Mexico and back without being seen." Apparently the sheriff there received reports of a man riding a horse along high mountain ridges in the isolated Los Piños area west of the town, carefully avoiding traveled roads. "I wasn't doing anything illegal, but the sheriff arrested me on suspicion," said Durand. The sheriff brought him into town with his saddle horse and packhorse. He was held for investigation, booked as "Earl Duran," but was freed when a check of his fingerprints in Washington showed no criminal record. "He kept me in jail for a month for no good reason. They also arrested me in Arizona, Globe, it was. They took my guns away then let me go. I needed those guns to survive. I hated lawmen ever since."

It took all Riley's effort to keep his mind on the road. The two of them were quiet the rest of the ride.

MY WIFE, LORNA, AND I were in our parlor at the time, entertaining our friends Buck and Sue Buchanan and enjoying an evening cocktail.

I said to Buck, "You're chairman of the board, so you should be able to speak for the county commissioners on paving the road down to the house. I don't care what you name the road. Just put some asphalt down on it."

Lorna said, "Dear, save your business talk for another time. It's getting late. Let's decide on a restaurant and get on with dinner. I'd like to sit in front of the fireplace at the Half Moon and enjoy a nice rare steak. What about you, Sue?"

Suddenly there was a furious knocking at the back door. "What on earth!" said Lorna. "Please go see who it is, Milward."

"Hold your horses!" I shouted towards the door. When I opened it, in came young Robert Creager, all excited. Sputtering, pointing in all directions and starting over at least three times, Robert only managed to say, "Mr. Simpson, he broke jail…I saw him take a deputy with him in a car. You were the first person I thought of…I drove as fast as I could."

"Hold it, hold it. Calm down and tell me what happened." After he did, I said, "Buck, we'd better run over there and see what's going on. Sorry, ladies. It looks like dinner will have to wait for another time."

My wife calmed the boy down, gave him a snack of something to eat.

Buck and I rushed over to the jail. Over in a locked cell was poor Mr. Knopp, his head buried in his hands. He glanced up, grief written in every feature, but he didn't speak. Oliver Steadman rushed in seconds after Buck and me.

Then we put our heads together to figure out what we needed to do. Steadman and I were lawyers and the three of us knew the county government pretty well. We set ourselves up in the sheriff's office and got to work. But it wasn't so easy. There were lives at stake and we were novices at law enforcement.

"First, we need to call Powell, get hold of whoever is on duty at the sheriff's office up there," Buchanan said. He got on the phone. I overheard his side of the conversation.

"This is Buck Buchanan. I'm at the sheriff's office in Cody. Who am I talking to? Lewis? We've got some trouble down here with that young guy we arrested yesterday from over your way, Earl Durand. He just broke jail here and took a deputy along with him." Chuck Lewis told him he was on duty with "D.M." Baker. Buck said, "Durand's got three more felonies on him now—assaulting an officer, escape from jail, and abduction." Then Lewis asked him something. Buck answered, "Yeah, Noah's injured pretty bad. Durand slugged him over the head with a milk bottle." He paused then said, "That's what we figure, too." They talked about some details, Lewis giving Buchanan directions.

He hung up and said, "They'll mostly take over from here. I'll bet anything Earl will go home."

Lewis told us to have the telephone company put out a line call—a general alert to residents. I called the operator and told her who I was and what I needed. She said, "Sir, I'll have to turn this over to my supervisor. Hold on for a moment." A minute later on came the night supervisor. She said, "You'll need to compose your message and get back to me." I said, "We've already got it written." She took down the information and said, "In my eight years of working for the phone company, this is the first line call that wasn't about the schools being closed on account of blizzards."

Immediately a general alarm went out over the county telephone lines alerting ranchers and farmers about the escape and telling them to take precautions. In my mind's eye I saw folks taking down rifles, cleaning six-shooters, bolting doors.

Next Buck called the sheriffs' offices in Meeteetse and Greybull, which dispatched officers immediately. It would take a good hour for them to arrive, distance, night, and bad weather conditions considered.

We called KGHI in Billings, Montana, the only radio station Park County received. They broadcast a warning. The announcer reported what had happened and described Riley's car, believed to be heading toward Powell.

Soon D.M. Baker called. "Chuck Lewis and I drove the Cody road, but we didn't see Noah and Durand. They must have gone through before you called. Folks along the way will be watching for the car. We'll get calls when they see him. Any news?"

I answered, "We got the line call out and the announcement on the radio station." Baker said, "The call will bring in men to serve on a posse. Deputize them and dispatch them to hunt the roads." I said, "From what I hear, Durand'll make for the mountains. If he does, he'll need more ammunition and supplies. We'll keep a sharp eye out for Riley."

"Okay," Baker said. From what I can tell, that was the last word D.M. ever uttered over the telephone. "Okay," he said. But things weren't okay at all.

It didn't take long for the word to spread. Soon men started showing up at the jail to offer their services. The last volunteer to step up was Orville Linabary. I knew about him. He lived in Meeteetse, a small town south of here in the midst of sagebrush and sand, and just happened to be in Cody. He piped up and said, "If I had Old Betsy, I'd join up."

"Who's Old Betsy?" I asked him.

"That's my rifle the game wardens took away from me as punishment for killing six elk. Harry Hecht up at the lumberyard bought her. The judge auctioned her off along with the elk. If I had that gun and I'd get that son of a bitch in my sights, you wouldn't have any further worry."

I said to Buck, "Here's this poacher hunting another poacher. I don't like it a bit. It would be a big mistake to deputize this guy, with his outlook and attitude."

Buck said, "We need all the help we can get. If he can shoot, so much the better."

"No, Buck. We've agreed so far on what to do. We'd be making a big mistake."

"Neither of us has been put over the other," Buck said. I could tell he was irritated with me. I said, "There's too much at stake, and if one of us doesn't have confidence in a man then the other should respect that opinion."

Buck was miffed. I think he liked the idea of one poacher hunting another. He was getting carried away with the excitement and drama. I couldn't say that to him, but that's what I believed. I said, "Let's go out in the hall and talk this over." I knew it wouldn't do for us to argue in front of the men. We wouldn't have any authority over them if we did. Out in the hall Buck said angrily, "I think you're trying to be the big cheese here. No one put you in charge." He was right and it was a shame. In the heat of the moment we didn't foresee the need for one of us to be in charge.

I said, "By rights Oliver Steadman is in charge because he is the county attorney. One less man won't make all that much difference, and a man like Linabary will cause a whole lot more trouble than he's worth. Buck, we've been friends for a long time and we'll be friends for a long time to come. I'm going to put my foot down, and if you don't like it, that's just too bad. Now let's shake hands and go back in and let the men know we stand together on the decision."

Buck thought for a while and slowly moved his hand toward mine. I could tell he wasn't happy with me taking the upper hand in the matter, but he went along with it anyway.

We went back into the sheriff's office. I turned to Linabary. Now he had a deputy's badge on his shirt. "Where'd you get that badge?" I asked.

"Sheriff up at Meeteetse give it to me. I was on a posse for him once. He let me keep it as a souvenir."

"The hell he did," I said. "Durand's a better shot than you are. Your being arrested for poaching disqualifies you. I won't deputize you." That was the end of it as far as I was concerned. Linabary thought he knew better. He snuck up into the Beartooth mountains six days later and put himself right in Earl's peep sight, taunted Durand, and paid for it with a rifle slug in his heart and an instant death, the damned fool.

I swore in a posse of ten men. We conferred with sheriffs from the area. Because the county was low on law enforcement officers, with Riley gone and the sheriff on vacation, we assigned Dwight King to take charge of the manhunt. King had already been in on the first capture of Durand, bringing him in after the poach. He was an experienced game warden, knew how to lead men so that they would conduct themselves properly. Within an hour we talked with Sheriff J. R. McFate and Undersheriff W. H. Moore of Red Lodge, Montana, Robert Phyde, deputy sheriff from Bridger, and Sheriff Don Parkins from Basin. They drove to Powell to help out, meeting there later that night.

King stepped up to give his orders. "We'll get out to all the side roads. It's getting cold. If Durand throws Riley from the car, he might freeze to death. Then again, Durand might kill him, but I hope not. If you shoot, shoot to wound. So far Durand hasn't committed a capital crime."

As soon as the men received their instructions, they left Cody. A heavy snow had started.

AT THIS VERY MOMENT Chuck Lewis and Baker were having a showdown with Earl in the Durands' yard. Unarmed, Chuck approached Durand and said, "Give up, Earl, or I'll have to shoot."

Durand instantly turned his rifle on Lewis and fired. The bullet entered Lewis's left arm, passed just under his heart, and severed his spinal column. Then Durand shot Baker at the point of his left vest lapel, killing him instantly. Baker was near retirement age. He had a nice farm all ready for him and his wife to settle down on. He was a kindly old gentleman, honorary godfather to probably a hundred folk around here. Chuck Lewis died at the hospital a few hours later.

We hunted from trucks and cars from that Thursday night until Saturday. Having driven as fast as he could from California, Sheriff Blackburn arrived Saturday afternoon and took command. He ordered a search of places around the Powell flats that Durand was known to frequent, with no results. We speculated about where Durand might be. We were afraid he had escaped into the mountains. You might as well forget about finding a man like Durand if he wants to get away.

VIRGINIA TURNER

NEIGHBOR

I WAS A NEIGHBOR AND a close friend of Earl's parents, Walter and Effie Durand, and I walked into the story at this point. What I didn't see, I heard about soon enough.

They tell me when Earl and Riley arrived at the Durand farm, Earl said, "Turn the car around and point it toward the road. They're out hunting for me, but they won't take me."

Walter Durand had no idea who had driven up in front of his home. He came out of the house and walked toward the car to greet the visitors. There was no telephone in the house and the radio wasn't on. When Earl stepped out his father was stunned. "Earl! What's the matter? What are you doing here?"

"I had to get out! I couldn't stand it! I'd go crazy locked behind bars!" Then he ordered his father, "Now get my .45 automatic and the box of shells." He motioned with his revolver for Riley to get out of the car.

The elderly Durand looked at the man and asked, "Who's this with you?"

"Riley."

"The deputy sheriff? Give up, Earl! Go back to Cody. You can't get away with something like this. I won't stand for it! Go back and take your punishment like a man!"

Durand looked at the revolver in his hand. "Nothing doing. I'm not going back to jail—not alive, anyhow. I can't stand it. I'd go crazy in jail! Get in the house and get me my automatic." The three men walked toward the house. "I don't know where it is," his father protested. "Your mother's hidden it."

Riley staggered up the steps and onto the sun porch. Earl pushed the injured man through the doorway. Blood was caked in Riley's hair; there were splotches and trickles and smears of it all over his face. The blood around the wound was beginning to coagulate. Riley was in shock. He was about to faint. When Mrs. Durand saw this horrid-looking stranger enter her house, she let out a shriek. Then Earl stepped across the threshold and his mother was dumbfounded. Earl looked at her as if his visit should have been expected. He was keeping his anger under control, but he was sure angry.

Without a word of greeting or explanation, Earl said gruffly, "Mother, this is Mr. Riley. Wash his head and fix it up."

Though nearly beside herself with fear, Earl's mother brought hot water from the stove and washed the blood from Riley's head. Trembling with shock, Riley sat in a hard chair. As Mrs. Durand worked, her body began to shake with convulsive sobs. In the middle of washing Riley's face, the overwrought woman fell limply into a chair. Mr. Durand was already sitting, his shoulders drooping.

Durand towered above his father, who recoiled when he realized his own son was aiming a revolver at him. Earl's voice was sullen. "Dad, I'm not going to fool with you. Now get that automatic and help me pack."

Mr. Durand did as Earl said. Earl removed Riley's gun belt from the dazed deputy and buckled it around his own waist, slipping on his own gun holster to join Riley's.

WHEN I HEARD THE NEWS of Earl's jailbreak, I drove to the Durands' farm to warn them, in case they hadn't heard. I was worried that Earl might show up without warning. It was snowing. I didn't notice the car in the driveway. I was thinking about what my neighbors would soon be going through. Earl was a big disappointment to them, unwilling to work on the farm and leaving his father with everything to do. Since his escape from the game wardens and his arrest two days before, Earl had become their tribulation in this world. The three daughters were so gifted—schoolteachers, wives, well-spoken and well-thought-of. And Earl brought dishonor to the family. I felt for the Durands' suffering. I saw everything almost as if I was there. Jenny Blackburn, the sheriff's wife, was a good friend of mine, too, so I knew the jail from visiting her. My mind's eye filled with pictures of Earl's breakout. If I had noticed the car in the driveway, I would have put it together with Earl. I was so intent on my thoughts that I didn't notice the car at all—a thing that big!

Soon I learned what was going on inside. Mrs. Durand sobbed, "Here comes a car," fearing for her son's life.

Earl turned on Riley and said, "Get up and get out on the porch." Shoving Riley ahead of him with the rifle's muzzle, Earl stepped out to get a good look at the car pulling into the yard. Riley was hoping there was help in the car, other law officers or possemen.

Earl interrupted Riley's thoughts. "I'm going to rest this rifle on your shoulder. Don't you dare move." This was Earl, who had as steady and easy a shot as anyone could want.

Riley felt the rifle's weight and remained motionless. The muzzle jutted out about even with his chin. He must have imagined the deafening explosion of the rifle, the gunpowder burn and sting that would tattoo his face if Durand fired. They were invisible in the darkness of the unlit porch. Earl could instantly shoot down anyone coming from the car. Riley felt Earl's left hand, steadying itself on his shoulder, suddenly tense, and stifled the urge to shout a warning.

I stepped from the car. In the dark I couldn't see a thing. I walked up on the porch and knocked on the door. From behind me Earl asked, "What do you want?" and suddenly the whole picture became clear to me. "Come in," he said. I turned to leave, hoping to retrace my steps, but Earl stood between me and the way out, and repeated, "I said come in. What do you want?"

For some reason Earl didn't scare me. I just knew he wouldn't hurt me. He was angry, but not with me. He had come for something and he was going to get it. I said, "I came over to tell your folks about your escape, Earl. But I see they already know. Everyone's looking for you." Then I amazed myself with my own boldness. I said, "Go back to Cody and give yourself up. Get in my car and I'll drive you there."

Instead of getting mad at me, he spoke with sadness in his voice. "I can't stand it there! The air's dead! I'd die in there."

It seemed like jail or the loss of freedom scared Earl. In a few seconds he pulled himself together. And the three of us went inside.

"Go finish washing yourself up," Earl said to Riley. Earl went about his packing while Riley washed his wound. Riley was certain if he could stall Earl, help would be arriving soon. Riley suspected that Earl would hold him hostage until they reached the mountains. Durand went into a bedroom, closed the door, and changed his clothes. When he came out he was wearing Levi-Strauss overalls and a khaki shirt. Barefoot, he sat down with a gun in his lap and put on three pairs of wool socks, then a pair of four-buckle overshoes.

I spoke to Earl again, looked him right in the eye. I realized that he was a young man standing at the crossroads of life. I said, "If you don't turn yourself in, you'll regret it the rest of your life." I didn't realize the prophesy in my own words, nor did I have any idea how soon it would come true. At that very moment, a car entered the driveway. Its lights cut across the front windows and moved along the back wall of the living room. "Here comes a car," I said. We heard the tires crunch on the driveway gravel, the motor stop, and two doors open and slam shut. Earl turned away from me, his rifle cradled in his arms, and said to all of us, "That'll be the law." Then he spoke to his father. "Go out and tell them to leave. I'm not going back to jail." His mother just slumped in her chair, quietly sobbing and moaning, the life gone from the poor woman.

The night was pitch black. Earl said, "You go out there and send them away, or there'll be bloodshed." Then a voice I recognized as Chuck Lewis's shouted, "Earl! Come on out now with your hands up in the air. We're here to take you back to the jail. Mr. Baker is here with me. You can trust him. Nobody's gonna hurt you. You just have to go to jail and serve your sentence. If you come along peacefully, nothing more will happen to you. There's five men here!"

Still calm, Earl ordered his father, "Go out and tell them what I said."

Mr. Durand went outside, spoke with the law officers. We could hear most of what they said. "Earl said you should go away. He said he won't go back to jail."

Lewis spoke up. "He has to come with us. He's committed serious crimes. He'll only make matters worse for himself if he doesn't give himself up now."

"How is Mr. Riley?" Baker asked. "Is he okay?"

"He needs a doctor, but I think he'll be all right. As far as convincing Earl to come out, I wish there was something I could do. He's made up his mind that he's not going back to jail."

Lewis spoke up one last time. "Go in and get him, Mr. Durand, or we'll have to go in ourselves."

Mr. Durand came back in and said, "They say no, Earl. You have to go with them." Without another word on the subject, Earl said to Riley, "Pick up my pack and go to the door." Riley picked it up, carried it to the threshold, and put it down. Armed with a rifle, Riley's revolver, and his own automatic, Earl followed. Riley turned right, taking a few steps to the side into the darkness, hoping to lose Earl now that his attention was on the car. Riley did not reappear. Later I learned that he had slipped off to the Smith farm down the way from the Durand place. Baker spoke up. "It's me, D.M. Now Earl, put up your hands and step into the light." And the three of us inside, the Durands and me, sat and waited, listening.

As it happened, both law officers were in the glare of the car's headlights. Earl could see them easily in silhouette. Earl fired his gun, one shot, immediately followed by two more. He came rushing back into the house and grabbed the pack he had prepared.

"My God! What did you do?" asked Mr. Durand.

"It was them or me!" snapped Earl. "I'm going to the mountains where they won't find me. This is the last you'll see of me!" And he was gone into the darkness.

Mrs. Durand fainted and tears came to Mr. Durand. He pressed a bandanna to his eyes and just rocked slowly backward and forward in the chair. I looked at my wristwatch right after I head the gunshots, realizing that soon the authorities would ask me to testify about what I heard and saw.

"Mr. Durand," I asked, "Do you know where Mrs. Durand keeps the smelling salts?"

"Smelling salts? I believe Effie keeps them in the bathroom medicine chest."

I found the salts, wet a washcloth, and revived the poor woman, who was in a bad way. Even though I could see that the Durands were paralyzed by the horror of what was happening, I asked him to look at the kitchen clock and say what time it was. Seven-twenty, we agreed. Then I went through the house turning off all the lights. I sat on a couch in the living room, sat for I don't know how long, doing absolutely nothing. I could not hear talking or any noise whatsoever from outside. Finally I roused myself and asked, "Mr. Durand, where do you have a flashlight? I need to go outside and see what happened." I rummaged in the drawer and found an Eveready. Walter took the flashlight from me and we went out into the yard.

I heard moans of agony. Walter moved the flashlight beam around until he found Lewis wounded. I looked. Lewis was bleeding so bad that I knew it wouldn't be long before he would die.

Then Mr. Durand's flashlight caught D. M. Baker. "Oh! Baker, too! My God! He's dead." I'm not a woman with a weak stomach. I thought I could look at anything. I helped at the butchering of hogs and cows, but to see a dear old friend sprawled dead in the driveway and all that blood—I nearly fainted from grief.

Mr. Durand and I struggled to get Lewis into my car so I could take him to the hospital. Then I told him "I'm going to take you and Effie to my house. I'll fix things up for the night for you." I bundled the grief-stricken Durands into my car, drove to the hospital, helped get Lewis onto a gurney, then took them to my house. It was ghastly for them, for all of us.

Art Glasgow

Neighbor

WE KNEW THE DURAND family well, lived just two miles apart. The Durands moved to Powell the same time we did. We were Midwesterners originally. But back in 1908 my mother's doctors recommended a high, dry climate for her tuberculosis. My father, principal of the Jacksonville, Illinois, high school—in the heart of flat, black-earth corn-growing country—went to Wyoming to scout around for a homestead. He bought a place just north of Powell. Mother died two years later, when she was thirty-seven.

At first Dad and I farmed. Then I was busy hauling crops to market for the farmers during harvest season. I hauled sugar beets and beans. The Bighorn Basin grows most of the country's sugar beets. A lot of the sugar sold in America is from beets, not cane. I saw Earl Durand unloading trucks at the weigh station a few times. The beets are stored at railway sidings in long, flat-topped mounds, something like the famous Indian mounds back home in Cahokia, Illinois, except ours here are much smaller, more regular, and temporary. But there'd be dozens of those beet stacks alongside the railroad track, waiting to be hauled for processing to the sugar factory at Lovell. The beets give off a lot of heat and moisture as they sit in the out-of-doors. On early autumn mornings you'd see steam coming off the tops of the mounds. A sight to see, the morning sun obscured from view by these battlements of beets, the rays shining through billows of steam overhead.

In the winter Dad and I hauled coal and, at odd times, sand and gravel for concrete. After a time we had several trucks and employed a fair number of drivers.

I went to school with Laura and Ida Mae Durand, two of Earl's older sisters. I graduated with Laura in 1922. The family was well liked and well respected. Mr. Durand was a dedicated Mason. Several times he was elected Worshipful Master. Walter Durand and his wife Effie were pretty good-sized people. That's how come nobody was surprised when Earl turned out to be a six-foot-two, two hundred-pound bear. His real name was David Earl Durand. His father was David W. By changing the middle name, they avoided the "Junior." Mr. Durand built a one-story house on the east side of the road, planted windrows of trees for protection against the winter wind and for shade in summer.

Around here you have irrigated farming or you have no farming. By nature the Bighorn Basin is a desert. Buffalo Bill Cody's dam and Shoshone Reservoir with its vast network of canals ensure a plentiful supply of water. Irrigation made farming possible and profitable. On the Durand farm they raised a fair acreage of sugar beets, some hay, and beans.

Once or twice I went shooting with Earl, just target practice. One bright autumn afternoon back then, we hiked a few miles down the Powder River to a bend and a winding in its flow. The trees along the banks and their leaves—golden and red with combinations of both on the same tree—were that marvelous vision called "fall foliage." We shot at dead limbs and branches, shearing them off as close to the trunk as we could get.

Then Earl said, "Throw some wood for me to split."

I broke up some limbs and branches into foot-long pieces and when I collected ten or a dozen, I started lofting them for Earl. After a couple, Earl could see that I wasn't too much impressed. I knew the trick of what he was doing. He could tell just by watching my reaction. I didn't show a lot of enthusiasm, didn't marvel at his hits. What he was doing wasn't all what it appeared to be. To a novice it looked like he was shooting at a moving target, but it was really a still target because it was poised at the top of its arc. The third chunk of wood—no sooner did it leave my hand than a shot rang out and splinters flew in all directions. I learned Earl could hit a moving target as well as a still one. When he saw the look on my face, he let out a booming laugh. I said, "Earl, you proved your point."

Then he said, "Toss some of the sticks out over the water one after the other."

The second before each stick touched the water it would disintegrate and disappear. I had seen good shooting before, but Earl was the best I had ever seen.

In March of 1936 I had double pneumonia and my father was sick with influenza. Dad was sick, taking care of me, and doing the chores, all at the same time. The doctor came every day. He told the neighbors that I wouldn't live. My uncle George came to visit on Sunday. He said, "It doesn't look like Earl Durand's very busy." He got Earl to come over once a day and help Dad with the chores. Earl wouldn't take any money for it.

EARL STOPPED HERE FIRST after he killed Chuck Lewis and old D.M. Baker. Why, Mr. Baker was more of an honorary deputy sheriff, just a sweet old man who everyone respected, a dignified gentleman.

Earl visited with us a few times not long before all this. He had stopped in a couple of weeks before and once or twice in the month or so before that, just neighborly calls. "How you folks doin'? Just thought I'd stop by and say hello." That sort of visit. We'd chat for a few minutes then he'd say goodbye and leave. We did a lot of calling on folks that way around here. Just keeping in touch with the neighbors. Ordinarily when Earl came to somebody he knew fairly well, he would just tap the door with his rifle butt. People knew it was him. He always carried a rifle, it seemed like. You'd hear that tap-tap-tap, you'd know it was Durand. But this time he eased in the house without making a sound. I had just lit an oil lamp. The first sign I had of Earl's being in the house was when I heard him say, "Move the lamp." He wanted it moved away from the window so someone looking in wouldn't be able to make out what was inside. So I moved the lamp. Dad and I didn't know anything about what had happened at the Cody jail or at the Durand farm. The last we had heard, Earl had been arrested for poaching. So we were mighty surprised to have him in our house. At first his manner was calm, as if nothing at all unusual was going on. But it was, you could tell. I mean, beyond just knowing that Earl had escaped from jail. But Dad and I didn't say anything to

Earl, didn't try to engage him in conversation. We just listened to what he said and did what he asked. He held the sheriff's Winchester automatic rifle so he could swing it from side to side and shoot in any direction he wanted.

Earl glanced up at the pantry shelf in the kitchen. He said, "I want some butter and a box of Quaker cornmeal. But the main thing I want is your .30–.40." He had come for Dad's mint-condition Winchester, 1895. My dad had owned it a long time, brought it with him from Illinois. Earl was familiar with the rifle because on our outings he had shot it, handled it like the exceptional firearm it was. It had a receiver peep sight and a twenty-eight-inch barrel. It was a lever action rifle with a tubular magazine, and sweet to fire. Earl's old .30–.30 wasn't worth two spits in a mud puddle compared to Dad's rifle. Also, later we come to find out that Earl had a big order of .30–.30 ammunition waiting for him at the mail-order depot in Deaver. So that's why he lugged his old gun along with him. But even so, at that time you couldn't find a better rifle of any make or model than Dad's Winchester. Earl wanted it because he knew he would hit what he shot with it. He said, "I want that .30–.40. I'll get killed, but somehow I'll arrange for it to get back to you." Here it was a good eight days before he was shot and he was already talking about getting killed. To be honest, I thought even then that he had set himself on the path of dying, probably even before he was arrested. Why would a man escape being arrested for poaching, then go out the next morning and commit an even more serious crime? He was asking for it, is all I can say.

"Give me all the shells you've got," said Earl.

Dad went to the gun rack, picked up the boxes, and gave them to Earl. There were only a box and a half, about thirty rounds. Earl started acting desperate. "Where's the rest? What the hell is this? How come you don't have more bullets?" he wanted to know. He was agitated. "Hurry up, Art," he said to me. "They might be shooting in this house any minute now."

I asked him, "What's the matter, Earl?"

He almost cried. He said, "I got away from them at Cody. I killed two men. They came to arrest me."

Dad asked, "Earl, what happened? Sit down, boy."

"I warned them to stay away. They were gonna slip up behind the trees and close in on me. They thought they'd get the drop on me. I'm not going back to jail."

My father asked, "Who were they?"

"One was Chuck Lewis. I don't know who the other one was. I shot them and took off."

We were horrified, listening in disbelief. Here was our neighbor confessing to killing two men. We knew all the deputies. They were all friends and neighbors. Dad and I couldn't express our horror to Earl, though the fact of the matter is, he never pointed a gun at us and never threatened us. But you could tell he might kill anyone he came across, and since Dad and I were right there, we just contained ourselves and let Earl pretty much have his own way. Then he corralled the cornmeal, some honey, and a box of raisins, darted over to the gun rack, grabbed Dad's rifle, and dropped the shells in his pockets.

"I'm leaving the sheriff's rifle for you to return to him."

But for some reason that I'll never understand, I made a point of insisting that Earl take it with him. I said, "You have the sheriff's rifle? Take his rifle with you, please."

Oh, yes, yes, he'd take it away, he agreed. And he did.

Just before Earl left, he said, "The only right thing to do is report that I was here, but you should give me fifteen minutes." Earl must have forgotten or didn't know we didn't have a phone.

When he left, Dad said, "I'm afraid this isn't the last we'll hear about our neighbor."

I said to Dad, "Letting Earl pretty much have his own way was the only thing we could do. I'd have liked to have done more to stop him, but I think any threat would have excited him."

Dad replied, "You did excite him when you insisted that he take the sheriff's rifle with him. Are you out of your mind? He was wound up so tight, the least disturbance would have set him off and spelled the end for us. Are you crazy?"

We had to drive into town to get to a phone booth. The first thing I did was call D.M. Baker's house to let the law know what was going on. I was upset and a little confused by my encounter with Earl, a little mixed up myself. Mrs. Baker answered the phone crying and said, "Mr. Baker is dead."

I apologized and said I was sorry. Then I grasped it. D.M. must have been the other man Durand killed. What would Mrs. Baker make of what I said? I'm sure for both of us it was like being in a stupor. I didn't seem to know what to say and said the wrong thing.

I don't believe Earl spent more than a quarter of an hour with us, though it sure seemed a lot longer.

AN AGITATED BUNCH OF PEOPLE had gathered in town by the time I hung up the phone. They asked me where I thought Earl would be likely to go. He had told us he was going to the mountains. A few years before farmers in the area had been raising potatoes, and they all dug themselves potato cellars. I said, "Earl might be in somebody's potato cellar or in a haystack. I'm a little skeptical about his going to the mountains." I was quite sure there'd be slim pickin's up there, as far as finding Earl. He played hide and seek around here for a few days—dodging here, there, and yonder.

As far as I can figure, Dad and I were the last souls Earl spoke to until about five days later, when he started showing up at neighbors', getting food and provisions before he went up to the mountains. Between the time he left our door until near the end, he didn't see or speak with hardly anyone.

AT THE VERY END, WHEN EARL was robbing the bank, my father and I were out at a little creek west of town where we used to get pit-run gravel. We were loading a jag of gravel for a farmer who was going to mix some concrete. When we drove into Powell with the truckload, people told us about the holdup. Earl shot up the town, you might say. He had bullets flying up and down the street and everybody looking for a hole to hide in.

All that afternoon till late that night the town was a madhouse. All of Cody had come to Powell. It was more like a "doin's" than anything else.

Of course, later, I stopped by to pay my condolences to the Durand family after Earl's death. While I didn't approve of anything Earl had done, I visited for the family's sake and said, "If there is anything I can do in your bereavement, do not hesitate to call on me." Much to my surprise, they asked me to be a pall-bearer, and I was.

They didn't want any outsiders at the funeral, didn't want the curious and the morbid. Earl's parents were brokenhearted and just wanted to bury their son in peace, a quiet and dignified service. Late Sunday afternoon it was, at the Easton's Funeral Home. The Eastons carried out the family's wishes. About fifty mourners were present, including the family circle and a few neighborhood friends from northeast of town. The other pallbearers beside me were neighborhood fellas—Mr. Croft, Jack Turner, whose wife Virginia had been in the Durand house when Earl killed the two law officers, Earl's brother-in-law from Belfry, Montana, and a family friend from Lovell. Roses and flowers in sprays and wreaths and bouquets covered the casket and were placed about the chapel.

The eldest daughter, Laura, traveling by train from her home in Missouri—near the family home where Earl was born—got to Powell just in time for her brother's funeral. She sat next to her younger sister. All the ladies wore black mourning, with veils over their faces. The youngest sister couldn't get to Powell from New York City in time for the funeral. She reached the train depot on Tuesday, so Dad and I had to pay a second condolence visit. Needless to say, the funeral and the visits were uncomfortable for us, but we all have neighborly duties to fulfill, comfortable or not.

A couple of days after Earl was buried, Dad got a call from Sheriff Blackburn. He asked, "Are either of you missing a rifle?" Dad said, "Yes, Earl took my rifle."

The sheriff asked him to describe it and Dad did.

The sheriff said, "I'll deliver your rifle in the next day or so."

The sheriff drove over the next day with Dad's Winchester and a few of the bullets. Since sheriffs like to get re-elected, Sheriff Blackburn gave some to people around town and down in the flats, told them these were bullets Earl had carried with him. The sheriff told us, "Earl left your gun at the Herf Graham place. He gave instructions that it was to be returned to its owner. I wish he had been as scrupulous with human lives." Even though Earl hadn't fired the rifle, Dad spent a good deal of time cleaning it.

DICK SMITH

· YOUNG NEIGHBOR

WE LIVED A MILE AND a quarter from the Durand place. Earl was nine or ten years older than I was, and when you're sixteen, ten years is the difference between a boy and a man. I used to watch Earl. I remember the day he went by with three horses on his trek down the Rockies to New Mexico. I envied him and thought how exciting it would be to go. He told me he planned to do like the mountain men of old, the pioneers who carried very little with them but lived the life of the free man.

Sometimes Earl took me plinkin'. He'd come by driving his dad's car and invite Ronnie Knopp, me, and some other boys to go up in the hills where the shooting wouldn't bother anybody. Earl would carry a sack of old bottles. He'd line them up and teach us how to shoot. He furnished the ammunition. I learned to shoot from his pointers. He liked doing things for people.

The first time I ever went big-game hunting, Earl went with us. It was a bunch of neighbors. He killed all four elk and three of the four deer we got that day. Earl didn't think much about limits in those days, as long as there was no more than one carcass per man. If a game warden questioned us, we would say each man killed one animal.

We were hunting antelope one time and a blizzard came up. Because of the swirling snow, we couldn't get any game. We got down in a coulee to eat our lunch, and Earl said to another feller along, "Throw Dick's apple in the air and let's see if I can hit it." I think it was Ronnie tossed my apple up. In a second it was out of sight, lost in the snow. Then Durand just splattered the apple with a rifle shot. Some got on my coat. He was using a .30–.30. As a rule that's all he ever carried. He shot that apple. Earl let out a laugh and said, "Boy, that was luck. Try it again and let's see." Ronnie tossed the second one. I brought only two apples for my lunch, and he demolished both of them and everybody laughed. Their damned joke cost me my lunch.

Earl lived in a frame tent alongside his parents' house. I was in it several times. He spent the winter in it because he was accustomed to outdoor living and hated being indoors. He felt trapped, stifled when he was inside buildings for more than a few minutes. He hadn't slept inside his parents' house since he was sixteen. He was tough like a pioneer or a frontiersman. In the early spring he would gather his supplies. He didn't take much with him—salt, cornmeal, parched corn, raisins, and he would jerk a little meat of his own. In March he started getting in shape to go to the mountains. Many an evening Earl would run by and if I was out doing chores he'd wave at me. We had a good watchdog. He would bark whenever a man afoot went by. Closer to spring we might hear the dog bark three times. In other words, Earl jogged around a square mile three times—that would be twelve miles. That was the kind of shape he got into. If Earl started his run early enough, I might see him come by before dark on his second trip around. There were wooden bridges across all the ditches and creeks. One was right on our corner. After jogging the seventh mile, when he came to the bridge, Earl would jump up on the railing, run its length, jump off the other end, and there he goes. See what I mean? He had balance and agility. He wasn't just dogging along dead tired. He had a lot of energy to go it at a run.

As a rule Earl would return from the mountains in the fall and work to earn money so he could buy shells and guns and things he needed. Every neighbor wanted to hire him because he earned what everyone else earned, but he did twice as much work.

He worked for my dad many times. My dad hired a lot of men to pile beans and feed them into the threshing machine. Earl would also shock grain and do any kind of manual labor. I worked along with the crew and saw Earl shock all day and make ten or fifteen more rounds than anybody else. When the workday was over, he would stick his pitchfork in the ground and take off across the field for home on the run. He had that much stamina and energy.

Most young guys around here planned to take over the family farm. In school we studied agriculture and industrial training. You'd better know how to weld equipment, mix and spread cement, clear an irrigation ditch, and all the things farmers had to be able to do. You learned how to store grains and keep ledgers of sales and income. Everybody joined 4-H and, later, Future Farmers of America. He didn't mind day labor, but Earl didn't want to have anything to do with agriculture or farming. He helped his dad when he was home, but when he was needed the most, Earl was in the mountains.

Earl was a great fella in the things he did for people. He wasn't a mean man at all. His father was elected several times as Worshipful Master of the Shrine in Powell, and he also had a place in the Grange like all farmers did. The family went to church. Mrs. Durand was a great lady. She did everything she could for people. When I was in the third grade, Earl's older sister Ida Mae was my teacher. She married Mr. Harkins, an ag teacher who I knew well. Ida Mae used to come back to Powell and she'd visit with us.

THAT NIGHT MY FAMILY WAS sitting around the radio after dinner, listening to the farm prices and the weather forecast, when a bulletin came on the air. Earl Durand had broken out of the Cody jail. The bulletins told people to take safety precautions, lock their doors, and not let anyone in who wouldn't identify himself. Earl was described as being armed and dangerous, and that went without saying. The announcer described Riley's car and said they were probably going to Powell. For the rest of the evening, warnings about Earl were broadcast about every fifteen minutes.

My father, Otto Smith, asked, "When are you going to do the milking?"

"I'm on my way," I answered. I went out to the porch and put on my boots and coat. It started to snow that cold, mushy stuff.

I said to myself, "Earl will take the Willwood road. He'll figure the police are set up to stop him on the highway. He'll bypass Powell and drive right by here." So instead of heading right for the barn, I walked up the driveway toward the road. It wasn't long before Riley's car drove by.

I thought, "There they go."

Then I went to the barn. I milked the cows and put the milk in the cooler for the night. I wouldn't have thought of calling the sheriff to say I had seen Earl, but my uncle George Burke did. He was trying to be a law-abiding citizen. He wasn't picking on Earl. His call was how deputies Lewis and Baker found out where Durand was.

When I got back to the house, Dad was entering figures in his ledger. Mom was sewing. My sister was doing her homework. I sat down to practice locksmithing from a Crandel Correspondence School course.

First thing you know, at the front door there was a loud knocking. My mother said, "My God! It must be Earl Durand! Don't let him in!"

We all froze, terrified.

In a loud voice Dad asked, "Who is it?" Someone spoke. I couldn't understand what he was saying, but the voice told me it wasn't Durand. I said, "That's not Earl."

"Just a minute!" Dad called toward the door. In a loud whisper he told us, "Get out of sight! Go to the kitchen and stay there."

Dad unlocked the front door. In stumbled Noah Riley, soaked up to the waist, a nasty gash in his head. He was shivering with the chills and shock. He was out of breath and weak. "I'm a deputy sheriff—Riley."

"Come in and sit down." Dad helped Riley to the sofa. "Lie down, Mr. Riley." Then Dad called to us, "Come to the living room. I need your help." We came in and saw Riley lying there, badly injured.

Riley said, "Earl Durand is on a rampage. He just killed two law officers. I followed the light over your barn, jumped the irrigation ditch, and crossed the fields."

My mother's eyes opened wide with horror when Riley said, "He might have followed me."

Mom said, "Dick, go to the closet and get some blankets."

"Throw a few in the car. I have to take him to the hospital," said Dad. "When I leave, lock all the windows and doors. Turn out the lights. Don't answer the door for anybody."

Riley said, "Take a roundabout way in case Earl is laying for me along the road." He put one arm over my shoulder and one over Dad's. We helped him to the car.

I said, "Earl wouldn't hurt us."

Dad shouted, "You damned fool! You never know what a man will do when his mind snaps!" I helped Dad cover Riley with blankets to warm him up.

Dad drove Riley to the hospital in Powell. By the time they got there, Riley couldn't remember much of what had happened, couldn't connect the events. His speech was slurred, but he was trying to hold himself together.

The minute my father closed the front door, my mother and I locked everything. My little sister had all she could do to keep herself from crying. We tried to keep our minds off of the possibility that Earl could come knocking. That was on Thursday.

The next day, after people heard about the killings of Chuck Lewis and Mr. Baker, and what Earl had done to Noah Riley, they were afraid of what Earl might do to them. Pretty near all our neighbors left for town and moved in with friends. We done the same. With Earl around, people didn't want to be out on the farms. You never knew where he might turn up. For the kids it was a holiday, being away from chores and home for a day or so. But the farmers had to get up extra early to drive out to their farms to take care of the livestock. Even though Earl had nothing against us, we just didn't want to take any chances.

After a couple of days, Dad and I moved back home. We had the livestock to tend and the farm equipment to get ready for planting.

TIME WENT BY AND STILL no word about Earl Durand being caught. One evening, it must have been less than a week after Earl killed those two officers, I was alone at home, lying on the floor reading a magazine story. I heard a rifle butt knocking on the door. That was a sign Earl always used when he'd drop by to visit neighbors. Then Earl walked in. He was anxious, jumpy. "I need help," he said.

"Boy! Am I surprised to see you."

"You'll help me, won't you? I see the car is gone. Is anybody here with you?"

"No."

"Where are they?"

My father had gone in to visit with my mother and sister who were still staying in town. I didn't want Earl to know they were afraid of him so I told him they went to visit friends. I asked, "What do you need?"

"I need a razor. I'm gonna shave so they won't be able to recognize me so easy. I need scissors. Get me something to eat and food to take along."

Earl went into the bathroom, stripped to the waist and cut his beard with the scissors. Then he stropped a straight-edged razor sharp, lathered his face from my father's shaving mug, and talked while he shaved. "I'm going to the mountains. They'll come and get me, but I'm going where I can defend myself."

When he finished shaving, he tossed the scissors to me and said, "Cut my hair."

"I need to spread newspaper on the floor first," I said, and went out on the porch where we stored old papers. I came back in, spread out the paper, and started cutting. I had never given a haircut before. It's a good thing Earl wasn't too particular.

"They took Ronnie Knopp and put him in jail," I said.

"In jail? What for?"

"They thought he might know where you were, I guess. All I know is they arrested him and he hasn't been seen since."

"Those stinkers. Ronnie didn't know where I was."

I finished cutting. Earl didn't look too great, but at least he didn't look the same as he did before. The posse would have a hard time identifying him, especially since everybody knew him by his long hair and his big beard. As we picked up the newspapers and swept up the rest of the hair, Earl said, "I want your father to drive me out to the mountains. When will they be back?"

"They just left a few minutes ago, so I guess about eight."

Earl was getting jumpy again, impatient.

"That's too late!" he shouted. Then, disgusted, he said, "Get me some supper."

"I can't cook. Can you?"

"Just give me some sardines or tuna or something!"

I gave him a can of sardines. He opened it with his pocketknife. He sliced bread, drank milk right out of the pitcher, wolfed his way through a few other items. Meanwhile, I was gathering food for Earl to take along.

"Got any jerked beef or dried fruit or raisins or parched corn?" he asked.

Earl Durand shown in a photograph taken before he began his deadly escapade. This is the photograph that Dick Smith gave to Sheriff Blackburn. (Park County Historical Archives)

"'Bout all I got is more sardines, some apples, and pears. I could boil you some eggs."

"Okay, cook 'em up and pack me some fruit. I'll grab a few potatoes out of your cellar on the way out."

When Earl was ready, I lit a kerosene lamp and led him out to the root cellar. "Just throw some in my sack," he said. "Tell your folks I was here and I forced you to do everything. I knew I had friends who would help me out." With that, Earl ran off into the darkness. I heard his footsteps go off in one direction, but I'm smart enough to know that he was just giving me a way to direct the law if it ever showed up. Which it soon enough did.

Before long up drove the sheriff and some deputies. He asked me to lend him a photograph he heard we had of Earl. I found it and gave it to him. Then I told him Earl had just been at the house. And off the sheriff went.

THE MANHUNT

One man against the world is the situation up in the Beartooth
mountain country of northern Wyoming. Earl Durand,
outlaw, killer and mountaineer of prodigious skill, is holed
up in a natural rock fortress ... trapped on the mountain.

Denver Post wirephoto caption, March 25, 1939

Ed McNeely

Guide and Posseman

ME? WHAT DO I HAVE to tell about the end of Earl Durand? I wish I could say on the subject of Durand's last eleven days, you can't pry my jaw open with an iron bar. But that plain isn't so. I've got opinions on Earl's actions. I've got opinions about Frank Blackburn and the general running of things; I've got opinions about myself and opinions about opinions. I'll give you some; others you won't even know I have.

Let me warn you before we go too deep into this. I have a reputation for being a gad-awful liar. See this pistol with carving all over the handle and the barrel? Butch Cassidy gave it to me. I was with him and the Sundance Kid at the Hole in the Wall. I've told that to every school kid in Cody and every dude tourist that ever shopped in McNeely's Saddle Shop. Not one was ever inclined to believe me. Every one of them was disinclined, downright disinclined. Now, do I strike you as being a dishonest man? I got a reputation as a liar, so you'd better check what I say with "authorities" on the subject. For all you know, I might be blowing smoke rings and soap bubbles your way. Be careful of what I say.

Vern Spencer and me and most of the possemen knew everything there was to know about the mountains. We were reared here, same as Durand, hunted, guided hunting parties—the cream of the crop, illustrious names—through this part of the world from childhood on up. And I'll tell you something plain out. Durand could have escaped into the mountains and never been found again, ended up anywhere from New Mexico to Canada if he'd wanted to. He could survive in the mountains. Even if he were to run out of ammunition he could snare small game.

The Jim Owens cabin was the headquarters for the hunt for Durand in the Beartooth mountains. Durand was inaccessible on the mountain. (Park County Historical Archives)

I cowboyed with Durand. Once in a while Earl worked for Harry Sandler; I was Harry's ranch foreman. When Earl was cowboyin' he'd stay in the bunkhouse. On occasion he'd just stop by, stay the night. One night when he was staying with us in the bunkhouse, he got up at two o'clock in the morning. I happened to wake up. Maybe it was a little sound Earl made, I don't know. Earl went out, and I never seen any more of him. Durand just disappeared. I knew the man wasn't okay. I wouldn't ever ride ahead of Earl on the trail. Riding behind you, he'd shoot, and a tree limb would fall on you. That, plus the blast of a six-gun or a rifle going off just behind your ears. After he did it to me the first time, I always rode behind him. I've seen him pull his prank on other guys. This was Earl's idea of a joke, a harmless way to scare hell out of you. That limb would startle a guy, and Earl would be bellowing laughter.

Earl could shoot all right; he was good with the six-iron. I've seen him rattle a shock of grain, rouse a mouse—unholster his six-shooter and nab that little mouse. In the fall the barns would swarm with mice, like in the Farmer Brown cartoons at the Teton Theatre in Cody. Earl'd tear up the barn, turning it into his own private shooting gallery or hunt club. Boom! And another mouse gone to mousie heaven. I think that's good enough shooting, bad light and all.

Not that Earl was a bad guy and I was perfect. I had my share of flaws and vanities. Me and Vern Spencer took ourselves to be two of the handsomest bucks and smartest all-around fellers back in them days. During the summer all the guides and outfitters went cowboying. Me and Vern hired out to the dude ranches as much as we could. Good food, soft living, and entertaining the ladies. We were having one hell of a young manhood. We were more rakes than anything else, dude-ranch versions of all the cowboys of the screen. But we were sociable. Earl wasn't. That's mainly where we differed from Earl Durand. And we'd been mighty careful not to kill anyone.

My sidekick, Spencer, always said I was a sour clown. Suck a sourball and try to smile and that's about like me, he'd say. We were both recruited, Vern Spencer and me, for the posse. Frank Blackburn himself swore us in. Hand-picked, we was.

It was Monday, March 20, when the sheriff located a team of police-trained bloodhounds at the Colorado State Penitentiary in Cañon City. They got to Cody on Tuesday. The guy who ran the dogs was a top-notch officer. Angel was his name. A feller he called Trusty took care of the dogs—groomed 'em and fed 'em. He was a prisoner they trusted, a forlorn-looking critter. Looked like they jumped out of the funnies—Mutt and Jeff. Trusty and Angel. I handled a lot of dogs myself, had a reputation as a good dog man around here. Frank knew about my fondness for dogs; he told me I was going to be his link to Mr. Angel.

I said, "Frank, is this all you brought me here for?"

"I know you, Ed. You were hoping for some glory. We're here because a wanton killer is loose. We're not here for the glory of it. You kids never cease to amaze me."

"Kid? I'm twenty-six."

"Ed, you know how old Durand is? He's twenty-six, too."

The sheriff sure could be enlightening when he wanted to. "I'm no better than a dog, am I, Frank?"

Frank chuckled and said, "Quit your joshing and get out of here. Maybe these dogs will find Durand for us."

WHEN THE DOGS ARRIVED the hunt began in earnest. Before we went out to hunt for Earl, the sheriff had the courtesy to call on Earl's parents, console them, tell them what we were going to do. Mr. Durand invited Frank and me and Mr. Angel in. We spoke privately. Trusty waited outside with the dogs.

"Mr. Durand," says Frank, "I'm Sheriff Blackburn." The two men shook hands. "This is Mr. McNeely and Mr. Angel. We're hunting for your son." Just then Mrs. Durand came into the room. She had heard what the sheriff said. A look of terror and sadness swept over her face, and her eyes brimmed with tears. She held a handkerchief to her eyes.

Frank continued, "I have hounds now. Can't you get Earl to come in and give himself up? If you don't, I'll have to hunt him down. I'm sorry to have to tell you, but Earl's giving me no choice."

Mr. Durand sadly shook his head. "It's no use. I don't know where he is and he wouldn't listen to me anyway. He wouldn't give up. You might as well start out." It was a sad spectacle. Mrs. Durand broke down in tears. You could almost see what she was seeing in her mind's eye—her son hunted down by dogs like a bear or a raccoon.

"I'll try to talk to Earl when we find him," I told them. I knew there wasn't much hope of that, but I had to say something. Earl had shot the two law officers in front of his folks. Lewis didn't even have a gun. It was an awful thing for them. They were heartbroken.

Frank and I searched Earl's tent for clues to his activities and whereabouts. I found a little soap sack and looked inside. "Frank, this sack is full of ivory elk teeth." Bull elk have two ivory eye teeth. It's an oddity, but it's true. "I hear Earl sold them to the Elks," I continued. Members of the Elks organization prize these teeth. They paid a pretty penny for them, had them made into watch fobs and tie tacks. Earl kept some of the meat, but he killed them elk up at Yellowstone Park for two teeth from each one. He would travel

Sheriff Frank Blackburn (left) and County Prosecutor Oliver Steadman. The weapons they display are probably not the ones Durand had with him. (Park County Historical Archives)

there in different jumps, spending a night here, a night there, and then he'd be inside the park and poaching to his heart's content. But most of his killing was up on the North Fork. A lot of guides saw him up there over the years.

After we finished looking around the tent, the sheriff said, "Have Mr. Angel bring in the hounds." In came the bloodhounds and they sniffed Earl's bedding and clothes to get the scent of him. Frank said, "Let's see if your dogs can do any good." The handlers circled the house and we all followed the dogs eastward. Frank stood by Mr. Durand. He asked, "What was your son wearing?"

Mr. Durand described Earl's clothing. At the last he said, "He had rubber overshoes on, buckle-up galoshes."

Angel said, "Too bad. It's no good. They can't find the scent through rubber." If we knew about the overshoes before the sheriff called the warden, we could have saved Angel and his dogs a trip. We worked the area anyway. The hounds picked up Durand's scent on a bush he must have brushed against, but that was all. It didn't lead anywhere. The three dogs were next to perfect—perfectly useless I mean. But the dogs were here, so there was nothing to lose by trying.

We returned to Powell. By then it was late afternoon. Even the sheriff was discouraged. We had some other tasks to attend to, so we forgot about the hounds and moved on to what else there was to do.

The sheriff had me take Angel and his Trusty to their lodgings and then we got a good meal inside us.

TUESDAY EVENING ME AND Angel met at the Powell police station. We were just sitting around, talking and waiting for orders, when we got the call. The sheriff said Earl was on his way to the Graham place. He had finally showed himself. We took off—I drove. Now Earl was "wanted, dead or alive." We caught up with the rest of the posse at the Smiths', ran the dogs a little, let 'em loose, and farted around in the weeds. We went on to the Graham place where Earl had just paid a visit. Then we found out Earl had made it to the Crofts'.

When we arrived at the Croft farm, there were two dogs tied at the gate, barking like all get-out, straining at their ropes. Nobody wanted to go past them. So I jumped over the tall wire fence to get into the yard. I saw a man scoot out the back door and cut around the corner of the house. I shouted "He's back here!" We had him in the headlights for a second. I couldn't get a shot at him before he was out of sight. The sheriff had made his way into the house to talk with the Crofts, see what Earl had done while he was with them. "Come on out quick, Frank! I just saw him." He didn't hear me at first. So I ran into the front room. I happened to glance out the side window and caught a glimpse of Durand in the yard. He was aiming a six-shooter at Frank. I grabbed Frank and jerked him behind the heating stove. He was surprised, caught off guard.

"Frank, you don't know how close you come to being shot! Durand was drawing a bead on you."

The Croft family hid in the bedroom as soon as Earl bolted.

WELL, DURAND GOT AWAY. We were too late. Somewhere in the neighborhood of seven o'clock in the morning we was down at the Blue Goose Diner in Powell getting something to eat. We ate and jawed, a huge breakfast spread out in front of each man.

While we was waiting for the waitress to bring our dessert, sipping on our coffee and chatting, here come a farmer. He seen Frank. He come over and said, "Excuse me, sheriff, I was told I could find you here. I took him over on the mountain, dropped him off by an old ranch cabin."

"Who? Durand?"

"Yes, sir."

"Your name, sir?"

"Oh, sorry. Thornburg. Arch Thornburg."

"Ed, slide over and let Mr. Thornburg sit down."

So I did. Down sits this old farmer, timid, old-fashioned, his hat in his hands before the law, a man who had just been terrified out of his wits by Earl Durand. He was a scared old geezer. The sheriff didn't bother to introduce everyone around the table. He got down to business.

"Now, tell me what happened."

The old man began in a whisper.

"Speak up, please, Mr. Thornburg. I can't hear you. You'll have to speak louder."

"He made me drive him in the car. He came in my house about four o'clock this morning."

"How did all this come about, Mr. Thornburg?" the sheriff interrupted. "Start at the beginning, please."

"The sound of someone coming into our bedroom woke me and my wife. We knew Earl almost all his life. It crossed our minds that it was Earl. We kept our eyes half-closed. Earl came up to the bed and touched me on the shoulder. He whispered, 'I'm Earl Durand, and you know the jackpot I'm in. Don't get excited. Follow my instructions and I won't harm you.'"

"He told us to get out of bed and dress. He wouldn't leave the room so we could turn on the light. He had a flashlight covered with cloth. So we had to dress in the near dark. He had my wife get him some bread and butter and a glass of milk, also in the dark. He ate it in a hurry."

Mr. Thornburg ended up, "Earl said, 'I have to get out in the mountain country and I need some help. Don't like to take you out at this hour, but I'm afraid I'll have to. I'm sorry, Mrs. Thornburg, but you'll have to come along. I can't take the chance of you calling the law.' He said, 'I know they will get me in time, but I want to get into the mountains where I can fight.' It was about four-thirty when he had us drive him to the mountains, about thirty-five miles up.

"He said to tell you we wasn't cooperating with him, not in cahoots with him. He wasn't much excited, but still you couldn't tell what he was gonna do."

Turning to us, Frank remarked, "Not in cahoots. Nuts. Earl's scrupulous about the niceties, and lax when it comes to the major points." Frank asked, "What was Earl carrying, Mr. Thornburg?"

"He had a knapsack stuffed full of food, a pair of overshoes, and a bedroll. He had a lot of rifles."

"How did he look?"

"He was clean-shaven. The last time I saw Earl he had a beard."

Then the old man perked up, got to talking on his own. "Earl had checked the gas in my car before he came in the house. He said that he wanted to put more in the tank to make sure I'd have enough to go all the way back into Powell to see the sheriff." He pointed a spoon toward Frank Blackburn. "He made me siphon gas out of my truck and use it to fill up the car's gas tank. He had me drive out past the fairgrounds so as not to go through town."

"Just then we were driving back and forth along the highway looking for him," I said. "Durand was smart to go the other way."

Mr. Thornburg went on. "Earl asked if we knew who he had killed. He knew he had killed Chuck Lewis, but he didn't know who the other one was. He said he was sorry he had to kill them."

The sheriff asked, "Anything else, Mr. Thornburg?"

"Earl thanked us, then shook hands with Mrs. Thornburg."

Then, turning to the old man, Frank asked the sixty-four-dollar question. "Which mountain, Mr. Thornburg?"

"I took him over on Beartooth Mountain. He had me go as far as the old road would take us. That was the last I seen of 'im."

"Beartooth. He picked a good one. I wonder where he'll be. But he sure isn't going to be at the Hole in the Wall, now, is he, Ed? Boys, you going with me? I guess you have to. You're the posse."

Our pie arrived. Nodding toward Mr. Thornburg, the sheriff said, "Waitress, a mug of coffee, please, for our friend here. Piece of pie? Get Mr. Thornburg a piece of pie. What'll it be?"

Just as you'd guess, the minute he had a chance, the farmer orders a slice of banana cream pie.

Before he raised his fork, Mr. Thornburg folded his hands, like he was gonna pray. Instead he says, "Mr. Sheriff, I hate to say this to you, but Earl told me to." And he paused, unable to go on.

"That's all right, Mr. Thornburg. You go right on and deliver the message." The sheriff was always polite, courteous in his speaking. He was always a gentleman, not like us uncouth varmints. We were on good behavior when it was called for, but no longer than necessary.

"Earl told me to go tell you where he was. He wanted me to tell you, 'If you got the guts, come and get me.'"

Frank took a napkin out of the holder and fiddled with it, finally folding the paper into a little square. You could tell he was thinking. We kept quiet. Finally he spoke up. "Well, now we know where to find him. You guys may not have the guts, but you also have no choice. Finish up and let's head out." Another good jab.

While he ate, Mr. Thornburg said that Earl had told him where he'd hidden all those days. He had been in some willows along Bitter Creek about a mile from the Durand farm.

We all took our last forkfuls of pie and slurps of coffee, got up from the table like a bunch of Keystone Kowboys, stumbling all over each other, and stood around the cash register settling up our checks. Every face had a toothpick sticking out. You'd never think, to look at it, that we were on our way to hunt a man. It seemed like any other early-morning soiree at all the Blue Gooses everywhere, it was that ordinary.

The sheriff extended his hand to the farmer. "Mr. Thornburg, thanks for the information. I would appreciate it if you would drive out with us, lead us to where you dropped him off. After that if there's anything you need, we'll be glad to help you. I imagine Durand gave

Possemen in front of the Jim Owens cabin are armed and ready to hunt Durand. Their instructions: shoot and shoot to kill. (Park County Historical Archives)

you and your wife quite a fright. Then you should go on home and treat yourself to some extra sleep. We'll find Durand soon."

SOON A CONVOY OF CARS AND trucks headed out and drove to where Mr. Thornburg led us, the old Jim Owens ranch. As if by magic, armed men began to gather from all around. This went on for a couple of hours. How they heard where we were, I'll never know. It was something to see. The sheriff was surveying the scene and doping out a plan, talking with the posse he had brought with him around a little fire I got up. First thing he did, Frank sent me to shepherd eager volunteers out of harm's way and out of earshot. A lot of the men were sent by sheriffs' offices from all around the country. He talked with some of the men who made their way to camp. Some of them he kept and some he kept in reserve; some he sent off to the side. He ended up with seventy-two men, including those of us he already had working for him.

Two of the guys started acting like they was the posse. They was talking big and fine. One of the cowpokes took a bottle of whiskey out of his coat pocket. It was Orville Linabary, a guy who had tried to get on the posse back in the beginning. As I heard it, Milward Simpson wouldn't swear him in because he had been convicted of elk poaching himself just a little while ago. "Here, have a slug for good luck," he said to his sidekick, a guy named Argento, who joined him.

Then Linabary said, "We'll get that bugger's scalp. It'll be just like hunting a big dumb bear out in the open."

He was a regular speechmaker.

"I'm going up that dry creek bed. I bet he's up around that boulder. Who's coming with me?" Linabary asked. The other dumbo looked like he'd be game.

I spoke up. "You fellers sit right where you are and don't move. You're all right now, but one step in the direction of the mountain without the sheriff's say-so and you'll land your butts in jail."

The "leader" mounted his horse, took a rifle from its scabbard, and smart-alecked me. "Who the hell do you think you are?" he asked. "It's a free goddam country." Then he said to his friend, "Let's go hunting!" Argento got on his horse, too, and opened his big yap. "He killed two law officers, two neighbors."

"He's no better than a skunk. We aim to get him," said the lunk Linabary.

I ran up and grabbed the horses' bridles. "You ain't going nowhere. Now get the hell down off these horses. The sheriff's running things, not you damn clowns."

I noticed that Linabary had an official-looking deputy's badge on his shirt. I said, "Take that badge off. You ain't no deputy."

"It's a souvenir," he protested. But he took it off and slipped it in his shirt pocket. He must have known the sheriff could arrest him for impersonating an officer.

Dick Holler, one of the possemen, ran up. "Frank is giving orders. He's coming over." Then Dick told the horde, "The sheriff is coming over to talk to you." When he said that, the wind left those two clowns like they was a popped balloon.

Immediately up come Frank, his sheriff's uniform perfect in every particular, trademark Stetson fixed firm on his brow. He spoke to the men dying to be sworn in, but who he was going to send home.

"Men, I am pleased to see that you are willing to do your civic duty. That is honorable and I express the county's appreciation. I have sworn in all the posse I'm taking with me. I can't watch out for people who have no business on the mountain."

Smart-guy Linabary piped up again. "We have business on the mountain with Earl Durand."

Frank answered quiet, but all the men heard him. "For your sake, get off the mountain or you'll sit inside a jail cell. Now get out of here." Then he spoke up and addressed the group. "From this moment on, and until further notice, it is against the law for anyone who is not on the posse to be on this mountain. If you're caught, you'll be arrested and thrown in jail, just like Durand was. I thank you for coming and hope we see each other under more pleasant circumstances. Good day to you." Frank turned to me and said, "Ed, see to it that everyone gets safely off the mountain."

So that was my assignment. I was walking the kiddies home from school, a goddam safety patrol. When I finished I went up with the dog handlers to look for Earl.

Once we got in the hills, Angel gave Trusty the run of the dogs. "Now, don't try to slip away from the dogs," Angel joshed. "I don't want you joinin' up with that Durand and making us have to deal with a gang of desperadoes." Low humor, and Trusty didn't get it. "Trusty"—that's all I knew him by. Us dogs went up on the north side of Littlerock Creek. Frank and his bunch trekked right along a creek beyond a ridge on the south flank of Beartooth. Boyd Bennion led a group up the south ridge.

Me and Angel and Trusty was out all day down in the meadow below the mountain. It was a waste of time. See, Durand was smart in some ways and stupid in others. He was smart enough to wear rubber overshoes. The bloodhounds couldn't get a scent, and me and Angel didn't accomplish much more than pass the time of day. But Earl wasn't smart in the ways that really count. He could have been anywhere in the Rockies he wanted in a day or so. But he decided to stick around and get himself killed. He went to some lengths to see that piece of work finished. The man wasn't right.

From where we were, we couldn't get a shot at him, let alone see him. There's a place where the mountain ridge fades into the sweep of the mountain wall. On the south slope there's a rock, standing like a turret midway down a four-hundred-foot-long talus slope. A sparse, scraggy stand of timber—broken trees, busted logs, limbs, and branches—surrounds the rock. Earl was somewhere in there. A steep slope drops away from the rock, commanding the slide below. This was where Boyd Bennion was with the possemen he led. Maybe Bennion was gonna catch the same criminal twice.

Suddenly we heard two rifle shots, real fast. That was all. Then the posse started plugging away with rifle fire toward where the shots had come from. When Durand began shooting back, it suddenly seemed to those guys like there wasn't a boulder big enough to hide behind. Earl set up there and laughed at them, 'cause he could see them, but they couldn't see him. Come to find out, when we got back to camp, Durand had killed those two idiots I had discouraged down below. Those knuckleheads were begging for it—why, I'll never know. It had come to this: Earl didn't care how many people he killed now.

It got dark and Frank had us come in.

THE NEXT MORNING FRANK said to me, "Ed, we're going to send the dogs back. They can't do any good. A lot of folks round about are going to drive up here like this was a circus carnival. I want you and Dick Holler to go down to the creek crossing and turn the cars around." He was laying on the importance of the job, so I knew it wasn't worth much.

I said, "Here we are in the mountains, and I'm assigned to directing traffic. Frank, I thought you held me in higher regard than that."

"We don't need any sightseers around here," Frank said. "Now get the heck down the hill and watch the road."

Two days later—after the National Guard was posted and the posse was searching for Durand—we got an air-mail letter from Bill Monday telling us Earl had made his way to Powell and had been killed! The sheriff sent me on ahead to town to find out what had happened and keep law and order. I ran down, jumped in my car, and took out after the desperado.

That wasn't exactly the end of it. The sheriff wanted to find the place where Durand had hidden. He had a few of us bushwhack around on the day Durand was buried. We found the hideout in a willow-covered bottom of Bitter Creek. Durand had left behind a quarter of raw beef and a leg of venison. Where he got them from, I don't know. Here was a bed roll, two pistol holsters, a knapsack, two hunting knives, needle and thread, a tube of healing ointment, and a bottle of iodine. I wonder why he didn't take some of this along with him. He sure could have used it. But who knows what Durand was thinking by then.

I'M GLAD I HADN'T RUN INTO Durand after cowboying with him. The world is filled with enough fools and cowards, and those that ain't cowards are often fools. There are few occasions when it pays to be courageous, and facing Earl Durand wasn't one of them.

Here's my business card. One side is just the name and address for McNeely's Western Wear, Cody, Wyoming.

I only give the box number. Sometimes I deal with customers who I might not want to find their way back here on foot, but who I don't mind doing business with through the mail. Snots and such. It's the back of the card people get a kick out of, one of them smart-aleck things I'm famous for hereabouts:

A Man Has 27 Parts That Don't Work

20 Nails That Won't Nail
2 Tits That Won't Milk
1 Belly Button That Won't Button
2 Balls That Won't Roll
1 Cock That Won't Crow
1 Ass That Won't Work
What Are You Smiling About?
You Have A Pussy That Won't Catch Mice!

But don't worry about it. I'm the butt of my own jokes, too. In the bathroom at the store I have this sign up so's anyone sitting on the pot can read it.

Notice

All Employees are required to take a bath
before reporting to work. Since we have
to kiss your ass to get you to do anything,
we want it to be clean!

Signed: The Management

Since I'm the only one works here, it applies to me. I must have given away a million of these over the years. Some get insulted, others take it as a joke.

Vern Spencer

Guide and Posseman

I GOT AN EARLY START at the rugged life. I was born in Telluride, Colorado, when it was a mining camp. The way my mother told it, she started feeling funny and she hollered at someone going past. Whoever it was came in, gave her a hand, and all of a sudden, there I was. She said I was born smack dab in the middle of a grizzly bear track, which explains my wildness. There weren't any doctors anywhere near Telluride. The family moved to Cody when it was sagebrush and rattlesnakes. Buffalo Bill was building the Irma Hotel and my father was hired to decorate the interior. Dad loved the country around so much that he bought a dude ranch up on the South Fork. I started wrangling and guiding at "Spencer Wigwam" when I was twelve years old.

I knew Buffalo Bill. My father owned a shooting gallery on Sheridan Avenue that attracted the tourists during the season. I shot there every day and ran the place for my dad. In the fall of 1916, eight men including my father trekked to the top of Cedar Mountain west of Cody. You could see the town from there and look west into the most beautiful mountains you'd ever want to lay eyes on. Buffalo Bill picked the spot where he wanted to be buried. He didn't end up there, but that was the place he picked. He owed a feller some big debts so the man got the Colonel's body to pay it off. He operated it as a popular tourist attraction outside of Denver, made big money off of Buffalo Bill's bones. The Colonel was gosh-darn good to me, awful big-hearted. He gave me a rifle of his, which I always treasured.

My usual line of work was as a guide, trapper, and outfitter during the season and a cowpoke the rest of the year. I know all the mountains hereabouts, know them well enough to attract a wealthy clientele. Mr. William Wrigley—of Wrigley's Spearmint Gum, Wrigley Field, and the Chicago Cubs—and men of his sort and stature. If a guide leads you to trophy game, you want your friends to see what a success you are at finding the best, so you recommend the guide.

Mr. Wrigley was an organizer, a real go-getter, and he wanted everything just so. He'd hunt with his cronies for a month at a time. Not only did they want to bring home trophies, they all enjoyed hunting for the table every day. It took a lot of game to feed a dozen fit, hungry men. Mr. Wrigley was the first out on the trail every day, the last in each evening. All the enthusiasm he brought to his work showed up on the trail. His love of sport was infectious. Sometimes he would bring along a friend who wasn't much of a hunter; by the time the guy left, he would be an ardent outdoorsman.

But my favorite customer was a younger fellow who fancied himself a sport. He boxed some, fished, hunted. He boasted that he was a great writer. I don't know anything about that now, because I never read anything he wrote. But he was a fair hunter. A client expects his guide to have a pretty good line of gab, especially a hunter like Hemingway, who was as much a big-story hunter as a hunter of game and trophies. I guided for him after the Durand incident.

I knew Earl some, and none of it was any good. He used to come up the river and shoot all the time. Once in a while I passed him on the trail. Earl was an awful poacher, violating every particular of the wilderness code, no regard for it whatsoever.

I owned a cabin on Aspen Creek. One time I was camped up near there and heard shooting upstream. Hunting season was over and as far as I knew, I was the only person around. I crept up and discovered Earl with a crippled doe and two wounded fawns. I said to him, "Gosh dang it, that's no good. What are you shooting a doe and fawns for, you danged fool? Don't come up this creek again. Hell, this is no good, Durand." I had to hunt around to find the animals and finish the three deer off.

I had no use for the guy. As far as I was concerned, he was a low-down skunk, with no regard for anyone or for the ways of the wilderness, in spite of all the time he spent in it.

In the course of a day Hemingway and I talked about everything you could think of. During a week's hunting I fed him bits and pieces about Durand and his last eleven days. It caught his imagination. He came back to the story again and again. He would bring up the subject with a question. He was thinking about the events. Finally he said, "That Durand story would make a hell of a good novel."

"You gonna write it?" I asked him. "If you do, you owe me a chunk of the money. If it wasn't for me, you'd have never heard of Durand." I was just joshing him, the way fellas would. 'Course I wouldn't mind having some of his dough, but that wasn't the main idea.

"No, I'm not going to write the book," he said. "Critics would think I was writing about myself again, just telling another blowhard tale. Besides, in some ways I'm too much like this fellow Durand."

"You even look like him, Hemingway."

"No kidding? How so?"

"Same build. You're both bears."

Then Hemingway said, "I once wrote a letter to another writer, guy by the name of Fitzgerald. I wrote, 'Invention is the finest thing but you cannot invent anything that would not actually happen. That is what we are supposed to do when we are at our best—make it all up—but make it up so truly that later it will happen that way.'"

"To tell you the truth," I said, "I don't know what the hell you're talking about, but if you know, that's good enough for me."

"What I mean, Spencer, is that this 'wild man of the mountains' story happened just the way a writer would make it happen. It's a little on the spooky side, if you ask me. I'll stay away from it. There's plenty of other stories to write out of my own imagination."

On that hunt Hemingway and his buddies bagged some fine trophies, mainly elk and bear. Afterwards he sent me copies of his books, but like I said, I never did read anything but the remarks he wrote to me on the front page.

A FEW WEEKS BEFORE EARL escaped from jail and started killing people, he broke into my cabin and stole some food. He cooked himself quite a feed, left my skillet up on the hill in back of the cabin, left it right in the fire. I found the skillet soon after, still in the hot ashes.

Earl also stole a knife from me—a beautiful bone-handled hunting knife, a gift from a company president I had guided on a hunt. Then Earl crossed the creek to Bob Rumsey's place, broke in, and stole eight guns. When the game wardens caught him at Rattlesnake Mountain, he had my hunting knife strapped to his belt. Earl was never prosecuted for those break-ins and burglaries. He traded the guns under the name of "Ray Rayburn" to a mail-order company in Salt Lake City for the three hundred rounds of .30–.30 ammunition. On his way to rob the bank in Powell, he picked that ammo up in Deaver at the express office! After all this died down, Bob Rumsey got every one of those guns back from the company, and I got my knife back from the sheriff's office.

SHERIFF BLACKBURN RETURNED from California late Saturday night and immediately got to work. He deputized me along with the first bunch he gathered, and I was never relieved of duty until it was all over. I was twenty-eight at the time. Some men the sheriff let go after a day or so, then brought others on to take their place. But seven of us he kept on from start to finish. I guess he knew we'd stick to it with the right amount of cussedness and he could count on us to tend to business.

The first thing the sheriff wanted to know was, had Durand shown himself yet. He hadn't. The sheriff said, "I don't think it will be too long before he does. He'll probably be looking for food soon." He called together all the guys who had been working on the posse. He told us how much he appreciated the way we had conducted ourselves and how we brought credit to Park County. He was good at public speaking, knew how to put folks at their ease, how to make them feel good. Then he said, "I'm going to cut most of you fellows loose now. I can't take the chance of having any of you killed by this murdering wild man." The sheriff was one to call a spade a spade. "I'm going to pick a few of you, put you on Durand's trail, and stay on it till we catch him." Starting Sunday morning after the sheriff returned, the seven of us left in the posse kept up a patrol of the country around the Durand farm. We drove up and down every highway and road within about ten miles of the place—and that was a stretch of territory—till something better to do came along.

We came off the road and reported to the sheriff at noon. Frank said, "I got an anonymous tip. Ronnie Knopp went into a hardware store and bought a hunting knife and cartridges for a .30–.30 rifle." We figured that the kid was buying Durand a replacement, since Noah Riley had taken Durand's hunting knife—which really was mine—when he arrested him. "Knopp was the boy on the elk poach with Earl. The caller said Knopp was buying those things for Durand. The boy may be perfectly innocent, but I'm going to take him into custody." Frank sent me along with Jimmy Dutton and Boyd Bennion to haul him in. We told him his father wanted to see him. The second he sat down in the car, I slapped the cuffs on him. Boy, was he steamed, stewed is more like it. Of course, he said he bought the equipment for himself.

BLACKBURN HAD BEEN TRYING to find a picture of Durand to circulate to law enforcement agencies throughout the county. So far no luck. Then early that evening, Tuesday, March 21 it was, we got word that Dick Smith had a snapshot, and we set out to get it. At least we had something to do until Earl tipped his hand.

We drove up to the Smith house. The sheriff knocked on the door and Dick came out. Frank said, "I hear you have a snapshot of Earl Durand. I need to borrow it for a while."

"I'll get it for you." He came back in a few minutes with the picture. The plan was, we'd head back to Ray Easton's funeral parlor. Ray had a darkroom and cameras. He'd make copies of the picture, and we'd get them to the local police and sheriffs' offices, game wardens, the Forest Service, and the FBI.

As he handed Frank the picture, the kid said, "Sheriff, Earl was here."

"Why didn't you call the police?"

"Earl told me to wait. He left a short time ago. I was gonna call soon."

"What happened?"

"He ate, took some food, and said he was going to the mountains. He was acting wild, talking wild. He made me cut his hair and he cut his beard off."

"Which way did he go?"

"He set off in the direction of the Graham place."

"Okay, son. Give me the picture and I'll make a phone call." Frank rushed into the house, called in to the office, and had McNeely drive out with Angel, Trusty, and the dogs. The sheriff came out. He ran over to us and said, "Durand was just here. I knew our luck would turn. I knew he would show himself. I wish there was some daylight. The dark of night is a bad time to go hunting Durand."

I chimed in, "The first time, he escaped from the game wardens because it was night when they stopped him."

He shot back, "Well, you're an encouraging sort, aren't you?"

We were all getting a little testy.

We took the picture along, but we didn't think much about it now. We had what we really needed—Earl. We fanned out from the house in the direction of the Herf Graham place. When the hounds arrived, we set them out into the field, but they couldn't pick up any scent. So we drove to the Graham ranch. When we reached the house, Mr. Graham was waiting at the front door with a rifle in his hand.

"Sheriff, I've been trying to get ahold of you," he shouted before we got to the door. "Earl Durand was just here. Me and the missus were sitting in the living room listening to the radio when I heard the door open. I turned around and there was Earl Durand grinning down at me."

"Earl was walking around, heading for the room where my father is asleep. I told Earl to stay out of there because my father wasn't well. Earl was courteous. He said in a neighborly way that he was sorry my father was sick."

Mrs. Graham joined us, drying her hands on her apron. "I said, 'Earl, what on earth are you doing here?' He answered, 'I want that new .30–.30 Winchester of Vern's and ammunition to go with it.' Vern is our son."

Mr. Graham added, "I reminded him, 'Earl, you know Vern just bought the gun with money he worked hard for and saved for. You're not going to treat a friend that way, are you?'"

"I got no choice," he told me.

"I saw he wasn't fooling so I gave him the rifle and a box of ammunition. We've known Earl for years, but I never saw him the way he was, determined to have his way."

"How did he act, Mr. Graham?"

"He was agitated but polite. He said, 'I'm in a jam. I expect to have to shoot it out with the sheriff. He'll get me eventually. I mean you no harm, and I hate to take Vern's gun, but I promise he'll get it back.' He sat in my rocking chair, took one of his six-shooters from his holster and set it on his lap. He said, 'The gun is out only so you can say you weren't helping me voluntarily.'"

"He left me this rifle," said Graham, handing it to the sheriff. "He said it belongs to my neighbor Mr. Glasgow and told me to return it to him. He also wrote down my son's rifle's serial number and gave it to me so I can claim it back."

The sheriff said, "Earl is trying to be a good neighbor and a desperado all at the same time."

"It's when you see a kid you watched grow up turn out this way…." remarked Mr. Graham.

"Did Earl say where he was going?" the sheriff asked.

"He said he had a couple more visits to make tonight, but he didn't tell me who he was going to see."

"Is there anything else, Mr. Graham?"

"Yes, sir. Several things. Earl wanted me to take him to the mountains. I told him I'd have to drive into town in the morning to buy some gas. He couldn't wait that long so he gave up the idea. When he left he said, 'I don't suppose I'll see you again, so good-bye and good luck.'"

Mrs. Graham spoke up. "Don't forget about the letter, dear."

"I was getting to that."

"What letter?" asked Frank.

"Well, he asked for a pencil and paper and sat right here and wrote you a letter," said the woman. "He worked at it a good ten minutes, I should think."

Graham handed Frank an envelope addressed to Sheriff Blackburn. In the corner he had written a return address: "Earl Durand, Undertaker's Office, Powell, Wyoming."

Frank opened the envelope carefully, unfolded the paper, and read the penciled letter to us.

"My Dear Mr. Blackburn," he read. "That was one dirty trick for you to jail those two boy just because I got away. If you sent him over the road I will kill you and that blankety blank district attorney if I live long enough and possibly can."

Frank looked up. "Someone along the way told him we arrested the Knopp boy." He turned back to the letter and read it smoothly and without emotion. It wasn't until I saw it later that I knew it was hard to read and had misspellings. "Tell King and Kennedy to always carry a pistol," he went on. "If I ever meet them I will give them a chance for an even draw—something I won't give you if you put up those boys. Tell that man whose beef I killed that if I live long enough to get back in the mountains that he has nothing to fear from me, I hope I never see him again. When you get after me better take about 20 men for your bodyguard and put braces on their knees."

All the stuff of a braggart, a chest-thumping nobody. But then the letter ended with some of the strangest prose ever penned by a man on his way to face down the law. I'm sure there isn't much else like it in the annals of crime and criminal detection.

Frank continued reading, "Of course I know that I'm done for and when you kill me I suggest you have my head mounted and hang it up in the courthouse for the sake of law and order.

"Your beloved enemy Earl Durand. P.S. I know where King lives and he may expect me around any time to shake hands."

When the sheriff finished reading nobody said a word. No comment was called for. We all knew that this was no time for wisecracks. It was best to hold our tongues. After a pause the sheriff said, "Well, at least we know he hasn't reached the mountains yet, and we have a chance to catch him if he hangs around here much longer." The sheriff stuck to business, and that's why he was the sheriff.

He let the hounds run one last time while we scouted the premises. No luck. As we walked back to the house, I asked Frank, "If Earl keeps on telling people that you're going to get him, why doesn't he just turn himself in and face the music?"

"Earl has a bigger exit in mind. We're just getting a taste of what young Mr. Durand will do. He's turned into a real desperado."

Then Mr. Graham hurried out of the house. "While you were out with the dogs, the Croft boy drove up. Earl had just been there. Mr.

My Dear Mr Blackburn.

. That was one dirty trick for you to jail those 2 boys just because I got away. If you send them over the road I will kill you and that Blanckety Blank district attorney if I live long enough and possibly can.

Tell King and Kennedy to always carry a pistol. If I ever meet them I will give them a chance for an even draw,—something I wont give you if you put up those boys

Tell that man whose key I killed that if I live long enough to get back in the mts. that he had nothing to fear from me, I hope I never see him again.

When you get after me better take about 20 men? for your boddy guard and put braces on their knees.

Of course I know that Am done for and when you fill me I sugest you have my head mounted and hang it up in the court house for the hope of law and order. Your he loved enemy
Earl Durand

The letter that Earl Durand wrote to Sheriff Blackburn. (Park County Historical Archives)

Croft sent the boy over here. Told him to warn me to wait until tomorrow to notify anyone that Earl had been here. Bob was so excited he could hardly talk. So now you know where Durand went from here."

The sheriff said, "Well, if the hounds can't take us to Durand, maybe his own threats will."

We was like the Keystone Kops and the Marx Brothers all rolled into one, chasing from farm to farm after this good-for-nothing.

As we drove off I said, "It's just like when he first escaped. He's getting supplies, collecting contributions."

By now it was about ten o'clock, and the Crofts' lights were already out for the night. We shined our headlights on the front and north sides of the house. McNeely and Dutton roared in with their car. They turned the spotlight on the house, too. Three sides of the house and part of the yard were lit. Sheriff Blackburn got out first and had us all wait in the cars. He went to the door and knocked loudly. No response. He rapped again and again, until finally a lantern was lit and moved over toward the window. Mr. Croft, Bob's father, came to the door, opened it slowly, but kept the screen door shut. He was nervous.

Frank said, "I need to see your son Bob. He was over to the Graham place with some information about Earl Durand."

"He's asleep. I don't know whether I can wake him," said Croft, turning away and leaving the screen door hooked. You could tell where his sympathies lay.

"If he's alive you can wake him. And before you leave you might unlock this door and let me in." The sheriff always was able to paint his expressions with a humorous brush when he wanted to, no matter what the circumstances. Croft came back, opened the screen door, and the sheriff stepped inside. "I wouldn't want you to think I'd been harboring anyone—willingly." Mr. Croft disappeared briefly, then returned. "Bob's dressing. He'll be out in a couple of minutes."

Then McNeely saw Earl bolt out of the back door—and vanish. We searched the yard. Nobody. But he was just here! As King swung his spotlight back and forth, the sheriff said, "He's there in the orchard! Get your light on him!" The spotlight caught the glow of some wild animal's eyes. King held the light on them eyes for a second, long enough so that when the sheriff got him pointed to the right spot, Durand was already gone. The sheriff cursed. "We'll get him yet! The only question is when."

Durand's luck held by a silk thread. Until now his thread held as good as hemp rope, but it wouldn't hold forever. Would Earl kill more innocent people, scare the bejesus out of folk? We'd get him, that was near certain, but for the moment we were all disgusted, coming so close again and again and him slipping away each time. There in the orchard—that was the closest we come to catching him. We was right on his heels, had him penned in that house and didn't know it. But he got away from us. We searched around the Croft place till six in the morning. No luck. The sheriff said, "Let's head in to the Blue Goose and get something to eat. If you guys are as hungry and pooped as I am, you need a break." We none of us protested. A cold night in March stumbling around farm fields. I'd had enough.

After Earl left the Croft farm, he barged in on young Harley Lee Jones. The boy was home alone. His folks were off visiting neighbors. Earl wanted ammunition for Vern Graham's gun and he knew that Harley had what he needed. It goes to show you, Earl knew guns, even knew his neighbors' guns.

This whole show was nothing but a bunch of smart guys running into one box canyon after another. We knew if we kept on we'd get Earl. We weren't concerned about looking good like all the law officers in Western dime novels and nickel story magazines. But nonetheless it wasn't no fun making ourselves look like monkeys time after time. I'm glad that this didn't happen during the summer when I worked at a dude ranch and specialized in spellbinding the gals in their twenties and thirties. My reputation would have gone out the window.

Next morning we learned that Durand had got himself a ride up to Beartooth Mountain. We went after him. That's where we'd catch him.

WE SPENT A FEW HOURS putting together a bigger posse. When we finally gathered everyone, the sheriff picked a dozen guys to lead groups of five who they got to pick. In all, there was seventy-two of us, including

McNeely and the dogs, Bill Monday with his plane, and a radio operator from the Forest Service. Not everybody went up the mountain. Some of the men worked on the cabin, setting things up. Some repaired the corral. The sheriff sent a few to watch the road. Sure enough, the curious started coming around to be part of the circus.

I knew tracking and I knew Durand wasn't up on the ridge where Frank took us. We cut across one gulch to another and there were no tracks on either side, so I told Frank, "Durand didn't go up this ridge." But Frank wanted to go up, so up we went. Frank was reconnoitering. I used to take that trail to Deep Lake Creek. There was no trick in finding out where Durand had gone. His tracks would head right for the middle of the mountain from where the Thornburgs had let him off. He didn't go up either ridge. It was a cinch. I would have done the same thing. There were four big pines downed in front of monstrous boulders and a growth of smaller trees and scrub all around. That was as good a spot as any, and that's exactly where Durand was.

We hiked quite a distance up the trail. Then we heard two rifle shots, quick, from over the ridge that rose to a knife edge thirty or forty feet to our right and about ten feet above our heads. Either Earl was shooting at the posse or they were shooting at him. We scrambled up the slope to the crest and peeked over the top. Even with binoculars we couldn't make out anything in the rock field below us. After running a few hundred yards downhill to find out what had happened, we ran into Stonehouse, from Bennion's group, struggling up to report to the sheriff as quick as he could. He gasped, "He got Argento and Linabary!" "Who's that?" Frank asked. "I didn't deputize anybody by those names."

"It's those two clowns you chased off the mountain."

That was all he needed to hear. The sheriff said, "Those guys are like ghosts. They've been haunting us all along. And they are departed souls now—ghosts. Come on!" he added, and we went, a little quicker, a little grimmer. All the groups started moving under the cover of a drop-off ridge below where the killing took place.

At the sound of those shots, a bunch of them scampered off of that hill like a bunch of jackrabbits. Some didn't even stop at the camp at the Owens place. They breezed by it and kept on going.

None of us in the sheriff's group bolted, of course. I said to Blackburn, "Look at that. There's your brave posse!" Most of them hung around the Owens place for fear of what Frank had in store for them. They were scared and Frank knew it. He wasn't going to do anything to them. There wasn't anything to worry about because now we knew where Durand was.

But it's a wonder I didn't get killed myself. I played lucky twice that day. I had a pretty good feel for the character and habits of the man we were tracking. I knew him and his low-down ways and figured out what he would do. After he shot Linabary and Argento, I suddenly turned dang fool enough to think I could get to him. I was struck by a crazy idea, I mean possessed by it. I once heard of a man who saw a mouse on his shoe and without thinking pulled his pistol and shot his foot. Too much quick-draw target practice. I stood my gun up against a tree and told Frank, "I'm going to talk to Earl. I know him." Before Frank could answer, I started up in Durand's direction and, by God, Durand cut loose. The bullet went through my shirt sleeve. I dropped down and rolled to get away. The next bullet hit smack right where I had fallen just the second before. Durand was trying to kill me. By rights he should have got me. That was my first stroke of luck.

The second came that evening. On toward dusk Frank, Bill Garlow, and me headed down the trail to call in reinforcements. We didn't know it, but Earl had cut out of hiding to ambush us along the trail. When we three stopped at a spring, I took my hat off and knelt down to drink. Out of the corner of my eye I caught sight of Earl. He was right there. He intended to shoot us. He worked the bolt and was raising his rifle. I shouted. Like jackrabbits, we popped up and hot-footed it the hell out, ran for the cover of trees and brush. I played lucky twice in one day. Kill us! Durand must have gone nuts. That's when the sheriff decided to call the posse in for the night for safety. There was no telling what Durand might do. He could go back to where he had been hiding. He could follow us down the mountain. He could find another spot to hide. He could try to make his way over the pass, but that was unlikely.

THE SHERIFF SENT MOST OF the posse home. He didn't need that many men for what he had in mind for the next day. First thing that morning the sheriff divided the two dozen of us he kept into two groups. Half were to block any escape route down the mountain and across the road. Sheriff Blackburn picked eight sharpshooters. He was determined to get the bodies out of there. He was quite sure that Durand was not where he had been. All along there hadn't been any sign of Durand. Though we were out of his line of vision and out of earshot, the sheriff sent one or another of us to take a peek with binoculars every once in a while over to where Earl had been. Frank led us up under the south ridge towards the place Bennion's group had been the day before. By now the story was so big, we had a gaggle of reporters following along. There was a team of Pathe Newsreel cameramen and a reporter, a *Life* photographer, and a *Denver Post* reporter. They were going to stop when we reached the bodies or when they got too tired to go on, whichever came first. At first, the "press" all kept walking out in the open, targets for Earl if he was still hiding in the same place. The rest of us, the posse, walked out of sight. Finally, all of the press except one Pathe cameraman got wise and joined us. When Frank told the young cameraman to get out of sight, he didn't. Then Frank said, "Young man, this is the second time I've told you to come down from the ridge." The guy kept taking movies of the scene. Finally Frank asked, "That camera belong to you or your employer?" We could hear Frank's wry humor brewing up a clever remark.

"Property of Pathe Newsreels, Sheriff."

"I hope they're not too hard on you if it comes back to them in smithereens."

"You gonna smash my camera, Sheriff?"

Several of us already had to stifle a snicker, and when we heard the kid's foolishness we all let the laughter slip, getting back into straight faces as quick as we could.

"Me? You young fool, you're a perfect target for Durand, just like a rabbit in a shooting gallery," was the sheriff's zinger.

Then I chimed in. "Stay up where he can see you. We'll use you for a decoy to find where Earl is hiding today."

Frank came back with, "You're dumb as an iron rabbit in a shooting gallery to walk where I told you not to. Just stay up there like Vern said."

The whole bunch of us got so involved in the joking that we had forgot ourselves and moved up into sight of the place where Earl had been. When we realized it, we scampered down like wolves were nipping at our heels. Then we approached again carefully, but we could tell he wasn't there because he didn't shoot at us. Even so, the sheriff sent in covering fire just in case. If Earl was still around, all the shooting would distract him. We found out that he was gone. It was a relief. Where was he now, was the question.

We reached the bodies. Argento and Linabary lay in a heap, stopped by a sapling. They had tossed and rolled quite a way down the slide. Sharp rocks had gashed their faces.

I noticed a couple odd things. Linabary's old deputy badge was gone and the rawhide lace was missing from his right boot. Earl must have had some use in mind for them. What the hell was he going to do?

Impersonate a deputy sheriff is exactly what Earl did with that badge. It got him his ride out while we was combing the mountain searching for him. And those laces. Later we found out what he used them for. But for the life of me I can't believe that when Earl unlaced the dead man's boots, he planned to tie up three bank employees with them.

KEN WHITTON HAD NO business being with us. The sheriff shouldn't have ever deputized him for the posse. He was a young, married feller. It was slow going up there—deep snow, fierce wind, bad footing. Accidents will happen. All of a sudden a gun went off and the boy let out a scream. We ran over to see what had happened. He was packing a tear-gas gun for the sheriff. The gas gun rubbed against his .38 six-shooter in his belt holster. His gun was old. The safety was worn and wiggled loose, and the boy shot himself. The bullet went in the back of his thigh, wobbled all the way down his leg, twirled and went down his ankle. I was carrying a first aid kit, but when I opened it all I found was a couple of aspirin. We built a fire, melted snow, and made the boy take the aspirin. That poor feller suffered something awful. We each had haversacks loaded with food, clothes, and a heavy blanket. We took the kid's blanket out of his pack, wrapped him in it, and carried him, one man to a corner. He was in misery. Every step we took pained him awful and it was a hell of a long hike down that mountain. It was a hell of a job, too.

The next day a doctor removed the bullet from the boy's ankle at Park County Hospital. Over the next few weeks his leg had to be sawed off three times. Within a month he died. Just another stupid mistake, a worn safety catch on an old six-shooter.

We spent the rest of the day hauling the dead and wounded down the mountain. We were at ten thousand feet where the air is thin. It was hard work. When we got to the bottom, there was Ray Easton's funeral wagon waiting for us. Easton's driver helped us zip the dead men up in rubber-coated canvas bags. One of the posse drove young Whitton to the hospital.

FRIDAY MORNING WE WENT back out after Durand—the sheriff and a dozen of us. We had food for three days, bedrolls, and one hundred rounds of ammunition each. We were ready to track Durand into the Clarks Fork if we needed to. This place makes the wilds look tame. The National Guard waited back at camp, ready to bring in the artillery if we found Durand in a spot where they could do some good. That never happened. Never needed them.

About two-thirty in the afternoon Bill Monday flew over us and dropped down a note in a manila envelope tied to a pillow. I ran over to retrieve it and carried it up to Frank. The sheriff read the note. "I'll be damned!" he cursed. "This says that Durand was killed at one-forty while robbing the bank in Powell!" We were stunned, couldn't figure how it could be. Had to be a prank. But there it was in black and white. Bill Monday wrote it and signed it himself. Stuck up here on the mountain, the reporters were afraid they were missing the big story down below. Before we started down, the sheriff took the possemen aside and said a few words, private. He told us he was grateful for the work we had done and sorry lives had been lost and that Whitton had been injured. Then we turned about-face and took off down the trail, jabbering away like magpies, like gossips.

Mel Stonehouse

Wrangler, Bronc Rider, Posseman

YOU KNOW, THEM GOOFY bastards, they're smart in a lot of ways and dumb in others. I'll tell you something about Durand. Me and Harold Siggins, we were out there on the South Fork one April. We had a couple of bear hunters up in the spring, hunting grizzly. There'd been a hell of a wet snow, about a foot and a half. This old boy Durand come in. He was wearing a pair of shorts. On his head he had one of them green eyeshades that clerks and bookkeepers wear, and his legs was wrapped in gunny sacks. He come in and we fed him. Harold was doing the cooking. Durand ate about three dozen buckwheat pancakes and drank about a gallon of tea. He was craving something sweet. Harold went into the kitchen for something. When he come back there was Durand with a tin plate full of syrup. He was just drinking it down. Harold run him out of camp, got himself a club and run him out. The old boy took off down the trail with them gunny sacks tied around his legs. Harold and me tracked him afterward to see where he had gone. About a hundred yards down the trail, he had turned off into the downed timber and just kept on going. So you know he wasn't too bright, wasn't all there.

In the fall I was working as an outfitter. I ran an outfit in the Thoroughfare. This wilderness begins at the point where the Shoshone splits into the North Fork and the South Fork. It comes all the way east to just west of Cody. This is a hunter's paradise, everything the serious hunter would like to bag. Some of the wildest country anywhere in the United States. Before hunting season you'd go in with a big pack outfit and you'd pack in everything that you needed for a four-man hunt. Usually that would take a string of two packhorses plus the one you'd ride. You'd pack in all the canned goods and staples; utensils you'd keep up at the base camp. A hunt would run two weeks to a month. We wouldn't bother for less time than that. There was a lot of demand for the longer treks, a lot of serious hunters. All the goods and gear would be packed in ahead of time because when you'd come down to meet your hunters you'd have so much stuff: their clothing, gear, rifles, and ammunition, and the fresh stuff like steaks and chops for the first few meals.

Well, I cached a big pack up at my camp in the Thoroughfare and about a week later I came back with my hunters. And here's this Durand, and what he hadn't ate, just like a grizzly bear, he had ruined. I run him right the hell out of there and told him I never wanted to lay eyes on him again. That happened a second time and I let myself get out of hand. I gave Durand a trouncing and that was the last he ever came around my camp. But that's how Durand lived. He had been poaching for years and I don't admire anybody who does that. I don't mind some old boy that lives up there in the country and goes out and gets himself a piece of meat. But when a man starts killing animals by the dozens, that's another thing. And that's what Durand was doing.

THE THING COME UP TO this: if Sheriff Blackburn had been there when Durand was arrested nothing would have happened. Durand must have thought he stood a chance against Noah Riley. Till the end of his life the poor guy was called "Milk Bottle" Riley. He couldn't live it down, but there was nothing he could do about it. Some folks forgot what his Christian name was after a while. But Noah Riley, he'd always been a peppery guy. When Durand was in jail, Noah couldn't keep himself from rubbing it in. He kept telling Durand, "Goddam, when you get your trial, boy, they're gonna throw the book at you!" Well, Durand, he caught claustrophobia in that jail cell. He wasn't gonna stay there. He was just like a little kid. He knew he was gonna get spanked bad.

Hell, when he finally got to court, they didn't do hardly nothing to him, fined him a hundred dollars and give him sixty days. He wasn't in as bad a jam, but Riley kept telling him he was. He was gonna go to prison for shooting that heifer calf, Riley told him. But I doubt it.

Frank Blackburn was one of my best friends and he knew Tommy Knight real well, too. In fact, Frank just about raised him and me. He was like a father to us. We were close with his son Frank, too; we worked the rodeos with him. All the young bucks tried their hand at rodeo. Some of us stuck with it, had a talent, a knack for it. Nineteen-forty-eight I was national bronc-riding champion, and in them days that was no small accomplishment. There were still real cowboys and you had to be damned good to win a national championship. When Tommy and me were in Cody we stayed at Frank's house—we bunked and boarded there. I was twenty-six at the time, same age as Durand. When all this started Tommy and me were out at a ranch in the neighborhood breaking horses. That's how come the sheriff was able to locate us right off. Frank had to form a posse right quick. He came out looking for us.

"I heard you two were out here playing with horses," Frank said when he found us. "I need you on the posse."

We started in joking right off. Tommy said, "I thought you'd 'a caught Durand by now."

I chimed in, playing like I was a little kid. "Aw, Frank, we was having fun."

But Frank was serious. "I don't have twenty minutes to josh with you fellers now. Raise your right hand and swear after me."

We were on our way. The fun was over.

The sheriff got every available man he could from all over that country. Me and Tommy, Frank, Ed McNeely, and another three or so other guys rode our horses from Cody over to the Clarks Fork and joined the bunch over there. They had repaired a corral and set out feed and water for the horses. I carried an aught-six. In this country you'd carry that or a .30–.30 rifle. Those were about all we used. The horses came in handy.

Durand was kind of stuck where he was. The pass he had to cross if he wanted to get out was buried in snow. It would be a difficult crossing to make, and nothing winters up in that territory except a few rabbits. He wouldn't have any game to catch for food. I was sure there'd be no escaping over the pass for him.

I saw Argento and Linabary get shot. I wasn't much behind them. I was with Bennion's group a ways above the rest of the men.

Four possemen pose looking in the direction where Durand was thought to be while another looks on from the doorway. The man on the left pointing his finger is Tex Kennedy and the man on the right is Harold Evans. (Park County Historical Archives)

We were pretty well scattered out. I heard them rifle shots, two quick pops, saw the two guys fall. I could tell exactly where Durand was. Boyd sent me over to tell Frank what had happened. I worked my way over as quick as I could.

After I told him, I asked Frank, "What now?"

He planned it all out in just a minute or two. He said, "We'll keep Durand busy from below. You and Tommy Knight run down and grab your horses, cut around the ridge, climb up to the crown, and get Durand from behind. It'll take you several hours. If you don't make it before you lose the light, stay up at the crown. When daylight comes, shoot him."

I said, "Shit, in this freezing weather?"

"As soon as we get him in our sights," said Tommy.

Frank said, "We'll keep Durand tied down tonight. Now you two get going."

After me and Tommy left, Frank gave his orders to the rest of the men.

It took us a long time to reach the top. We looked over the rim down into the canyon. It was already too dark to get Durand that night. After a few minutes, we noticed some lights moving down below. I asked Tommy what they were. He cussed. "Them son-a-bitches are taking off in the school bus like a bunch of goddam schoolboys. There they go!" Frank had driven the men up to the end of the road in a school bus he had borrowed.

I was calm at first, not near as agitated as Tommy.

"Frank didn't keep them up like he said," is all I said. But Tommy was just warming up. "What the hell! If he ain't gonna keep Durand in, there's no damn use of us staying up here freezing our asses off."

Then I got in the spirit of it. "Shit. I'll be damned if I'm staying all night for nothing."

We were just talking ourselves into going down. Tommy said, "Let's go. They ain't backing us up. They must have got a little cold."

I was downright indignant by now. "I'm disgusted as hell, I'll tell you."

We had Durand right behind that rock, or so we thought. That talus slope was shale rock, slippery. I don't care if only a rabbit went across it, you'd hear it. And we hadn't heard Earl move any rock. So we were pretty sure he was there.

'COURSE, WE DIDN'T KNOW we were wrong. Durand had followed the sheriff and his bunch down when they took off to tend to other things. As cold as it was, Tommy and I intended to stay up there all night just to snap the shot at him the next morning, after what he had done. But after we seen that bus take off, we said what the hell. We come down off the mountain about three o'clock in the morning. It took us that long to make our way in the dark.

The next day the sheriff took me and a bunch of other sharp-shooters to hunt for Durand again. 'Course, we gave the place a good going-over but didn't find nothing. We was just about as far away from him as we could get but didn't know it.

I would have given anything to have put my sights on Earl Durand after he killed them law officers. It would have been no different than killing a coyote or a grizzly as far as I'm concerned. It sums up to the same thing like with Billy the Kid. Billy the Kid was a goofy little guy. There was no way he could protect himself, so he learned to shoot. This was the same kind of deal. Just a completely goofy son of a bitch and they make a hero out of him. He wouldn't work, he wouldn't go to school. His folks were ashamed of him. He just did whatever he damn well pleased.

William Garlow

Posseman

I WAS SITTING IN THE restaurant of the Irma Hotel, the Cody land-mark my grandfather Buffalo Bill built and named for his daughter, my mother. I was stirring a cup of coffee, getting ready to enjoy a piece of apple pie with cheddar cheese melted on top. The radio was on, just the news and music of a mid-March Thursday evening. I took my first bite of pie. Over the radio comes this announcement: *"We interrupt this program for an important bulletin. The sheriff's office of Park County, Wyoming, reports the escape of Earl Durand from the county jail in Cody."*

Lucy, the waitress, came over and listened, too.

"Durand, a farmer from Powell, has taken deputy sheriff Noah Riley hostage. The escaped poacher is armed and considered dangerous. He is believed to be headed for Powell and his family's farm."

I was good friends with Lucy; we had known each other for years. We always joshed each other. I said, "I'd better get over to the jail and see if there's anything I can do." I took a last slug of coffee, then said, "You might as well eat the pie. Put it on my tab."

"What about my tip?"

"The pie is tip enough."

With her gum-cracking sarcasm, Lucy replied, "Thanks a lot, cheapskate. See ya later."

I slipped a dime under the coffee saucer, jumped up and ran to the courthouse. The only guys there ahead of me were Buck Buchanan, Milward Simpson, and Oliver Steadman. Milward said, "Hi, Bill. Come in. I'm counting on fellers like you to show up. I need to form a posse."

I said, "I don't know what the law is on something like this, but Oliver Steadman here is the county attorney and the only person I know of that's got any authority. If you'll deputize me I'll head out of here."

Milward said, "Raise your right hand and repeat after me."

I kept a room at the Park Motel in the east part of town—I spent so much time in town that I often didn't get back out to the ranch at night. Over at the motel I went to the closet, took out my .30–.06 rifle and twelve-gauge shotgun, and found two boxes of ammunition in the bureau drawer. Bringing them with me, I drove to my service station on East Sheridan and was filling up with gas when my closest friend, Morris Avery from Greybull, pulled in. Morris said, "I was up this way and heading home when I heard about the jailbreak on the radio. I came into town to see how I could help."

"I'm deputizing you!" I told him. "Come on, we got to get going." We got in my car and took off. Avery had a rifle with him. I said, "I think Durand will head for Powell and then swing around Heart Mountain. He has a sister living in the Clarks Fork area. I figure he'll go to her place after stopping at his folks' place. We'll try and catch him on his way to his sister's."

We drove out the unpaved country road north towards Belfry, Montana, and swung around the back of the mountain. We turned onto the road that goes from Powell and Ralston to the Clarks Fork and found a ravine with a little board bridge crossing over. I said, "I'll park the car out of sight. If Durand and Riley come over the hill, we'll shoot out the tires, then fight it out with Durand." Soon a farmer and his wife drove by. Morris and I stuck our heads up so we could get a look at the car. Having heard about the escape and catching a glimpse of the two of us in the ravine, the couple was afraid that we were Durand and Riley. The man tromped on the gas pedal and flew up the road—he looked nearly frightened to death.

We listened to bulletins on the car radio and stayed where we were until we heard Durand had killed two law officers. Then we went on into Cody where there were a lot of men milling around the jail. It looked to me like there wasn't going to be much to do for a while because there were no law enforcement officers around to give directions. I had training in this sort of thing, military training, but I had no authority to do anything.

There was talk about where Durand might be headed. Some believed he'd take to the Big Horns, which form a crescent toward the east, and the Hole-in-the-Wall country. This hideout, used by the likes of Kid Curry, Butch Cassidy, and the Sundance Kid, lies about thirty miles west of Kaycee near the Powder River. If Durand got into that country, he could stand off a small army for as long as his ammunition held out. Other folks thought he'd head west toward Yellowstone or the Tetons. Some others thought there were plenty of good hiding places around here.

But in a few hours interest petered out. Just a few diehards were left. We knew that help from the law would be coming in from the surrounding counties. So I let it go at that for the time being and went back about my business, hit the motel, and went to sleep. Morris went on home, as late as it was.

WHEN THE SHERIFF GOT BACK in town, I was called back into the picture. Frank Blackburn was getting a posse together after Earl had hightailed it to the Beartooth, and he called me up asking me to lend a hand. I said sure and drove on up to the old Jim Owens place. Frank had picked it as the posse's base camp. We were a few miles south of the Montana state line. The sheriff called me into the cabin to help plan for catching Durand. An operation like this needed planning or it could turn into a genuine disaster. We didn't jump the gun and just go after him. During the next few hours, we arranged food and bedding for the posse; set up a command post, a radio link, phone connections; rented horses, repaired old corrals, and took care of dozens of details. All Durand had to do was find a cozy spot and dig in, which is exactly what he did. Two points were in our favor: there were more of us than he could handle, and we had a pretty good idea of where he was.

About noon the sheriff gave us directions and final orders. He picked eleven of us to lead groups of five men each and he led one himself. Not everyone went up on the mountain. There were things to take care of elsewhere, and some of the groups were assigned to tasks and chores. I was disappointed that Blackburn didn't give me a group. I had military training from my student days at the University of Nebraska and was experienced in reconnaissance and tracking. I was a first lieutenant in the Army Reserve. Instead, Frank had me help plan the strategy and tactics. It wasn't much, not what I wanted, but I couldn't protest. He had too much on his mind and he was the ranking officer.

Just before we headed out, the sheriff said, "Caution is the word, men. Durand has killed before. Nothing will stop him from killing now."

The two groups were going up right behind steep ridges, one to the south, one to the north. I was part of Bennion's group heading up the south ridge. We had a pretty good guess where Durand was, and our group was the one likely to make contact with him. Just by surveying the scene, you could tell where Durand was hiding. About three-quarters of the way up the steep slope and in front of the thousand-foot-high ridge was a towering white rock, a natural fortress, like a turret, commanding the slide and slopes below. If Durand was behind that rock, he could stand off a small army single-handed. None of us was surprised. Durand was plumb ignorant in most ways, like killing two men, two law officers. But when it came to hiding and dodging, he knew the ropes. So there he was, out of sight, out of reach. There was no way we could get at him head on. Any fool could see that.

Following routes we had agreed to, the groups fanned out over the mountain's slopes covering both sides of Littlerock Creek, keeping under cover as much as possible. Durand was somewhere, watching our every move. Give him a target and he'd shoot it. That was how he was. Our group followed a sheep trail up the south slope of the mountain. We hiked for two or three hours to get into position and were fagged out from exertion. All along had been the quiet of the mountains.

Then Durand shot the two vigilantes. What those two lunatics Argento and Linabary had in mind I'll never know. They were the proof in the pudding that going onto the talus slope was suicide. But I can tell you, if I had been in charge of that group Argento and Linabary took off from, two less men would have died, and we would have stood a better chance of catching Durand.

When the sheriff reached Bennion, he took him aside and they had a conversation, a little on the loud side.

"What happened here, Boyd? I put you in charge. How come they went up?"

"Sheriff, I never saw them till they were out on the talus slope. They were determined. There was no stopping them. They're as crazy as Earl himself. They snuck off up in the trees then broke out running." Bennion continued, "First one of them—I think it was Argento—threw his arms up and fell backwards. The next second Linabary fell backwards, too. Then Earl started shooting over where I had put the men. It took us a while to make a safe retreat below the boulders and brush and beneath the ridge where his bullets couldn't reach us."

The sheriff said, "We can outmaneuver Durand. Stonehouse and Knight, I want you to trek up the mountain from the back. Take horses and cut around south to the next ridge. Get to the top as quick as you can." The plan was, if Knight and Stonehouse couldn't get up above him by dusk, they were to situate themselves so they could shoot him when it turned light enough in the morning. They didn't get far enough. As far as a good shot at him before sunset, why, it just didn't materialize. In our favor, Durand hadn't spotted Knight or Stonehouse.

After they set off, the sheriff said, "I want Boyd, Garlow, Spencer, and McNeely to work your way slowly toward the bodies. They might still be alive. We need to see if we can save them. We'll keep Durand busy with cover fire from the side." We snuck up over the ledge and into the boulders that lay between us and the open talus slope. No sooner did we get into the boulders than a volley of shots sputtered around us. He had us spooked. We fired at the rock where Earl hid. The whang and spat of bullets and the crack of rifle fire filled the air. We advanced slowly, skittering from boulder to boulder until we reached the edge of the open talus slope at the bottom of the rockslide. From there on it was just open space between us and Durand, suicide to go on. We kept up a steady stream of fire. We might have hit him by dumb luck. After ten minutes of this, Frank called us back in. "He's not going to let us through."

Spencer asked, "What are we going to do next?"

Frank said, "I'll tell you what we'll do. I'm going to have the National Guard send some men and artillery, and we'll also see what we can do about getting him from the air. I'll have Bill Monday's plane fitted out with bombs. If Durand is so smart, let him beat artillery and airplanes. We'll blast him out if we need to. And if he wants to surrender, we'll be there to bring him in." We were all surprised at his suggestion, but it was the only way we'd get anywhere against Durand. He asked the radio man, "Who's on the radio at the Owens place?"

"Name is Harry Moore."

"Get Moore on the radio and tell him to be ready to work tonight. We'll meet him there as soon as we get down from here. We'll work out of there and my office in Cody." We hadn't seen any activity from up where Earl was. When the sun started to set, the sheriff asked me and Vern Spencer to go down to base camp with him. Since I was trained in artillery, Frank put me in charge of the plans that had to be made.

We couldn't exactly determine the lay of the land on the mountain, so it was hard to know if Earl was staying put. Sure enough, as we went down toward base camp, he was waiting for us. He had worked his way down the mountain and planned a little ambush. But we must have showed up on the trail before he was ready. We spotted him, bolted, and made it down to some trees before he got a shot off.

Frank worried that Durand might sneak up on the rest of the posse, stalk them, pick off one or two, and disappear into the boulders and darkness. The posse made easy targets. As soon as we got to base camp, the sheriff radioed back and called the posse in for the night. He needed to protect his men. We hadn't planned this originally, so we had no way to let Knight and Stonehouse know. They would be okay up on the mountain by themselves.

WHEN WE REACHED THE base camp, Frank and I drove down to the Owens place to get on the phone. Harry Moore was already there. Frank went into Cody and I stayed at the cabin with Moore. Calls here and there got us in touch with Governor Roy Ayers of Montana. He had a National Guard Armory nearby in Billings. You can't just call a governor and tell him, "Send me one trench mortar, one howitzer, and shells to suit." But when he understood what the situation was, he said, "I'll gather my staff and put them to work on it right away." There were a lot of legal and technical points that had to be worked out. We were on the phone all night. There was a lot to it, rousing distinguished gentlemen from their beds, playing private eye, following up on folks' hunches where this man or that one might be, tracking down everybody from Senator O'Mahoney of Wyoming at a stag party in Washington, D.C., to the Secretary of the Army and the governor of Wyoming.

As it worked out, the governor ordered Adjutant General John Mahan to help Montana's Carbon County offices capture Durand. The order said, "This action is being taken for the protection of life and property in Carbon County in view of the fact that Durand's naturally fortified hiding place is almost on the Montana-Wyoming border. Durand's only apparent avenue of escape lies through Clarks Fork canyon and across the state line into Montana."

The National Guardsmen were deputized under Sheriff McFate of Carbon County, Montana. That was a formality. Frank was leading the operation.

Frank assigned me to be the liaison between him and the Guardsmen. I didn't know any of them personally, but they sure wanted to get to know me in a hurry. Being Buffalo Bill's grandson has its benefits and its drawbacks. Folks gravitate toward me like I'm a holy shrine. They want my autograph, photograph, handshake, slap on the back, and words of greeting. Well, with these guys it helped break the ice. An operation where you have the Guard working under the command of a sheriff is bound to be a touchy situation. I helped smooth that over.

IT WAS THURSDAY MORNING. Frank had me get in touch with Bill Monday, pilot and local glamour boy. The sheriff ordered him to fly to the Jim Owens place. When he landed, he had his new bride in the plane with him! Bill introduced her all around. He hitched up with one of them Hollywood starlets, a gal from Baltimore who lived in Casper. Her name was Joan, used to be Bedford. Joan Monday now. She had gone off to Paramount and made a few movies. She was infected with acting, a she-devil in her own right, and was used to the rugged life of Wyoming. Bill and Joan had been married for several months, since the end of the last year. She was a perfect match for Bill, but you couldn't tell how they'd do in the long haul. She was going to try to keep up her movie acting and come out to be with Bill as often as she could. You could bet he'd log a lot of flying time between here and California. He was handy with a plane. And he was handsome enough to make some movies himself if he wanted to. But for now they got each other's goggles steamed up pretty good just by holding hands.

The sheriff got Bill and me on the side for some talk while the plane idled. Not more than a dozen radio messages later, Frank said to Monday, "You're going to the Casper Armory. You'll pick up ammunition, and they'll outfit your plane with a couple of tear-gas guns and some dynamite bombs. They'll show you how to use them. You, the posse, and the National Guard, and we'll have him."

In mock complaint Bill said, "Gee, Frank, I'm on my honeymoon."

Frank came right back with, "No one told you to wait six months to celebrate your marriage."

BILL AND I WERE COMPETITORS, you might say. We both guided hunting parties for the rich. My clients were mostly serious hunters, big businessmen. He specialized in the Hollywood crowd. I said, "Frank, he'll do anything for publicity to promote his airplane tours and hunting trips."

"Well, he'll get his publicity now."

Bill overheard us. He said, "You're darn tootin' and I'm taking my bride along. This is part of our honeymoon, isn't it, honey," he said to his wife.

"Mrs. Monday, are you a daredevil, too?" asked Frank.

"Well, I should say not," she answered. "If you don't object, Sheriff, I'd like to run in to Casper with Mr. Monday and buy a few new dresses. There's a sale at the Kassis."

Frank said, "Just don't hold him up. I got a danged sight more important things to deal with than your saving a few cents on a dress."

Correcting the sheriff, she said, "Dollars. Besides, you can count on me, Sheriff. I'll have him back a lot quicker than if he was off on his own." She got back in the plane. Just before he took off, Bill turned to me to throw in a joke. He said, "I bet Pathe News and the *Denver Post* would like to hear about it. This would make a hell of a news story. Buck 'em off for now, will you, Garlow? We'll talk to them when we get back."

It was one of the jollier moments of Earl's last several days.

Now that Durand had killed two more men, the posse bivouac was swarming with the press.

Bill was right. Even though I didn't tell the reporters what Bill had in mind, they came up with the idea of an interview with Mrs. Monday on their own. They had a nose for human interest. I mean, for an angle that would sell papers, though there was plenty enough in the story of this man newspapers were calling Tarzan to fascinate the public.

The Mondays were back by eleven-thirty that morning. The plane landed in a small rocky clearing near the base camp. Frank ran over and said to Mrs. Monday, "Out of the plane, please, ma'am. I need someone up there who can drop some bombs. I hope you were able to get your shopping done."

She said, "I can drop the bombs as well as your posse. Deputize me."

Mrs. Monday was a regular surprise to us.

"All the bombs are right here under the seat. I worried that they might hatch, but they're okay," she said.

Frank was chuckling. "A female Bill Monday, I see."

But Frank was in charge. Bill stayed in the cockpit and Mrs. Monday got out. Frank said, "Bill, take Harold Evans along." Evans had been on the posse. Frank knew him and trusted him.

Bill flew over the area, combing every shrub, gully, and rock for a glimpse of Durand, concentrating on the rock where Earl had been the day before. Harold dropped the tear-gas bombs to force him out into the open—if he was still there. When Monday landed again, he said to Frank, "I can't tell if Durand is still on the mountain. We saw the bodies of the two men, lying sprawled on their faces. They're dead."

"You flew pretty low," said the sheriff to Monday. "You must have seen all there was to see."

Hunting Durand by plane, Bill Monday (left) piloted and Harold Evans flew with him. They hold a tear-gas gun and loads. Monday's plane was armed with dynamite bombs, also. They would try to flush out Durand if they spotted him. (Park County Historical Archives)

"Yeah, I got within a hundred fifty feet of the ground. We even flew between the canyon walls. If Durand had wanted to take a shot at us, it would have been easy. I'm afraid he's gone, where, I don't know."

THEN WE HAD TO TAKE Argento and Linabary down the mountain.

> *The King of France*
> *He had ten thousand men;*
> *He marched them up the hill,*
> *And marched them down again.*

You might say that's what we accomplished that Thursday. About the time Monday and Evans reported to the sheriff, three or four ravens appeared overhead and wheeled in narrowing circles, drawn by the corpses. Those birds have an uncanny sense for death. Frank took his rifle and fired a couple of shots in the direction of the birds even though they were too far off. "We'll get to the bodies before the birds do," he said. "There isn't much chance that Durand is still up there. We need to investigate and collect evidence. Our mission now is to carry down the bodies. I'm taking fourteen of you with me. I'm adding Emil Argento to the party." That was Arthur Argento's grown son; he had some little kids, too. The sheriff needed Emil to identify his father's body.

Then he called out the names of the men to go with him. He started with his son, also named Frank. Said the sheriff, "Your mother wants me to keep an eye on you, so you'd better come along." He named off thirteen more—Bennion and an assortment of skilled marksmen—and ended with, of all people, Breck Moran, the publisher of the *Cody Enterprise*, to pull double duty as sharp-shooter and on-the-scene reporter.

Breck asked, "You looking for good press when election time comes around?"

"Right now I need your gun more than your pen," answered Frank.

The sheriff had set out with the best sharpshooters he could find. Each man had one hundred rounds of ammunition, three days' food, and a bedroll. One guy lugged along a shortwave radio. It never worked. We were going to find Earl Durand—that's what we thought.

When we got to the place the posse had reached the day before, Frank turned to Boyd Bennion. "I want you and the men I leave here to lay down a barrage of gunfire ahead of us. I'm taking five men up there to the bodies and search where Durand has been." Frank picked me and four other guys to go on.

We set out and when we got to the edge of the talus slope, Boyd's men directed rifle fire toward the brush and fallen trees around it. We kept up a steady rain ourselves. The idea was to keep Durand busy staying out of the way of the bullets if he was still there. There was a blaze of rifle fire, the sharp tang of gunpowder, the cutting sound of the air pierced by the slugs and the zing and whine of rocks pinged and battered by the bullets. The rock splinters were more dangerous than bullets. The headwall of the canyon and the side caught the sound and threw it back, sometimes a second and third time in sharp echoes.

Our fire was not returned.

The sheriff divided the posse into two groups. Now, I did hear afterwards there was some talk that they didn't know each other's location. When the shooting started on one side of the canyon, the story went, the men on the other side figured it was Durand and shot back. No such thing happened. It was politics. You've got to remember, like Breck said, the sheriff is elected. Not everyone around wanted the kind of sheriff Frank Blackburn was. So someone concocted this rumor to take advantage of the press interest and present the sheriff in the national newspapers and radio as a bumpkin, not as the professional lawman he was.

We saw the bodies about one hundred feet below the white rock. They had tumbled down from where they had been when Durand shot them. They lay face down, held in place by a couple of saplings in a little patch of brush. The sheriff knelt without touching anything. "They were shot in the back," he said in disgust. "Small holes where the bullets entered. See? They must have seen him and were ducking for cover. Only a craven coward would shoot men down that way."

The talus was slippery. We sank into it. We skittered up, following the track the bodies made as they tumbled and slid down the slope. Fifty feet up from the bodies Frank said, "Look over here," pointing to two broken rifles, a .22 high-power and a .30–.30 rifle with a telescope sight. "Durand smashed those guns." Then he said, "Forty feet. He couldn't have missed at that range." I said, "He took their six-shooters and ammunition. He's a walking arsenal now. Just figure up all the guns he's carrying."

Then Vern Spencer said, "Linabary's right boot is missing the laces. But what would he want that stuff for?" He added drolly, "I guess Durand knew they weren't going to be doing any more walking."

"That deputy badge Linabary was wearing is gone," I noticed.

Spencer asked, "What the hell do you *think* he took it for, a souvenir?"

"Oh, I guess he took it so he can join up with us and hunt for himself," I shot back.

Even the quiet kid, Frank Blackburn, let out a peep. "Think he'll show for dinner and sign for his posse pay?"

Durand hadn't gone back to the rock.

The sheriff pointed to his son, Breck Moran, and me. "Come with me. We'll comb around the rock and see what's there. There's still a small risk that Durand is up there, though I think the tear gas would have flushed him out. But Durand is smart as a snake, smart enough to have us do what we're just about to do."

I remarked, "If Durand is up there drawing a bead on a spot twenty-five, thirty feet away he could mow down four men easier than drilling tin cans."

"So be extra cautious," said Frank. "The rest of you men start carrying the bodies down to the base camp." We were at ten thousand feet and several good miles from camp.

"Let's go," he said, and we clambered up the rock slide, charged around the gigantic boulder. We hunted and poked around. "Just what you'd expect to find—cartridges, food scraps," Frank said.

"I'm not surprised," I said. "I didn't expect him to go back to the same spot. This is where he was when he killed the two clowns. Where is he *now* is the question."

Frank said, "We'll go back down to where he got the shot off at us last night to see if we can track him. Garlow, you can help carry the bodies down."

YOU'D THINK WE'D JUST TURN around and march down that hill. We had gone a couple of hundred yards and all of a sudden we heard a gun go off right amongst us. Some poor fella lugging a tear-gas gun had it rubbing against his six-shooter. The dang thing went off and shot him in the leg. It's a good thing we had gotten some practice carrying Argento and Linabary those few hundred yards. Now we had miles to go and this guy to carry. We took a blanket out of his shoulder pack, four of us each took a corner, and we hauled him down the mountain, too. The difference was, the other two guys didn't feel a thing. They were already suffering from rigor mortis and this boy was in excruciating pain. The sheriff went on ahead. He hated to abandon us to the job of hauling down the carnage, but he needed to get down off the mountain as quick as possible and attend to the next problem on his hands, bringing in the Guard and hunting for Durand the next day. Seems like it was one misstep after another, but that's what you run into when you deal with a desperado like Earl Durand.

The sheriff went off toward where Earl had shot at us the evening before. He hadn't gone too far when he called me over. He stooped, pointed to tracks, and said, "Durand circled back and followed his own trail several times — the classic ambush. He would have ambushed anyone who discovered his trail and tracked him. This guy knows the game. We'll have plenty of trouble with him yet."

That's another point where the press gave the wrong impression. They kept thinking the only reason we were up on the mountain was to catch Durand. We had several reasons. For one thing, the sheriff wouldn't let the ravens get to those men before he did. Besides that, a posse is a damn expensive proposition. Why, when this thing was over it had cost Park County and the states of Wyoming and Montana $39,000 trying to catch Earl Durand. There was another point to consider. One more night and Earl could be over the Beartooth and into the fifty miles of Clarks Fork Canyon. We couldn't very well be hauling artillery over a snow-covered pass and back into the wilderness. We needed to stop him cold, right here.

We sent a guy ahead to have Harry Moore radio the undertaker in Powell and tell him that we had a couple of customers waiting for him. It was a discouraging day. You could almost feel that Durand was skulking around the place, just for the hell of it.

When we got back to camp, the convoy was there. They got into formation, had inspection, and in general put on a little show for us civilians. I didn't expect we'd see any use at all for the artillery. Now that would have been a performance the posse would have marveled at, a howitzer against Earl's rifle. If Earl had stayed put behind the rocks up on the mountain, we'd have had a display! But he wasn't likely to go back there again.

See, here's another area where the press got it wrong. They were reporting a posse of a hundred and a "detachment" of Guardsmen, painting a picture of maybe another hundred men. All together there weren't much more than two dozen us. Two hundred men on the mountain? That would have been a joke. We'd have been bumping into each other at every turn in the trail, and someone would have been mistaken for Durand and shot, that's for sure. Instead, by

The posse carried the bodies of Orville Linabary and Arthur Argento down the mountain. Les Cain, posseman second from the left, holds Linabary's laceless boot. (Park County Historical Archives)

now we were a small group of hand-picked crack marksmen, guys who wouldn't flinch at doing whatever needed to be done, from enduring fierce cold to shooting a man.

The plan was to carry the howitzer and the mortar along. Half a dozen of the Guard was going to carry them and the ammunition. Three were going to be assigned to one group, three to the other. Then there was going to be a couple in each group with rifles. A few would stay behind to man the radio and watch the trucks and gear. So there weren't too many of them actually on the hunt with us. This wasn't what happened. The plans changed. All the Guardsmen stayed in camp waiting to help if we found Durand and needed their firepower.

For all the traipsing around we did, not one bomb was ever let fly, The posse never fired another bullet, for that matter. But this wasn't a shooting gallery or even target practice. This was a time and a place where bullets were dead serious and to be put to dead serious use.

FRIDAY WE WERE OUT searching for Earl on the mountain again. The National Guard was ready to haul the artillery up if we spotted Durand. About two-thirty in the afternoon, we heard the roar of Bill Monday's engine. Bill came flying into view, flew toward us, circled around, and dropped something. When it hit, Vern Spencer ran over and picked up a fluffy pillow with a manila envelope tied on to it with some thick cord. He run it up to Frank. Frank tore open the envelope and read the short note. "I'll be damned!" he cursed. "This says Durand came into Powell driving a car, held up the bank, and is dead now along with John Gawthrop. I'll be damned."

Frank sent me and McNeely into town to lend a hand. Jimmy Dutton, too. Well, you couldn't have seen a more outfoxed bunch of scouts. If it wasn't such a damn tragedy, you'd 'a had to laugh.

THE

FREE RIDE OUT

KIDNAPPED BY RENEGADE KILLER.
HARRY MOORE ABDUCTED, then freed by Earl Durand
shortly before the wild man was shot to death in a Powell bank.
"Come to my funeral!" he shouted when he left Moore.
St. Louis Post-Dispatch wirephoto caption, March 25, 1939

HARRY MOORE

RADIO OPERATOR

The killer battered and tore windshield glass from Moore's machine because, "I don't want to be hit by flying glass."..."Be sure and come to my funeral," Durand called as he drove off alone.

Denver Post, March 25

IN '28 I WAS JUST A KID bumming around. I was passing through Cody on my way to the west coast and planned to spend a few weeks in the area, taking in Yellowstone, the Tetons, the Beartooths. I was low on money, so I asked about a job. The next morning I started working loading bentonite on a truck just outside of town. One thing led to another and here I stayed. Cody is as far as I got. Many Midwesterners settled here. The Durands were a Missouri family and I was from Iowa.

I knew radios and radio repair so after awhile I opened Moore's Radio Service. In addition to replacing burned-out tubes on folks' Philcos, Atwater-Kents, Majestics, and such, I kept up radio equipment for the U.S. Forest Service. Most of the officers who worked the Absarokas, Shoshone National Forest, and some other national forests in the vicinity had two-way radios. I had a contract to maintain and repair all those Forest Service radios.

When the possemen went after Durand, they were beyond the telephone lines. Sheriff Blackburn borrowed some Forest Service radio equipment. He said, "I need someone to operate this equipment. Who do you recommend?" The Forest Service said, "Get Harry Moore. He knows the equipment and he's a licensed radio operator." That's how I came to be involved.

My job was to transmit messages and reports for the law authorities. While the sheriff was on the mountain, my radio operation was at the Simpson place. John Simpson was the rancher taking care of the posse's saddle horses. His father, Peter Oscar Simpson, was eighty-five—no relation to the Milward Simpson family. He'd been one of the early homesteaders in the Bighorn Basin, moved in as soon as the irrigation canals and ditches began to run water into this dry valley. The few days I was there Grandpa Simpson never spoke at all, except to say "howdy" and "goodbye." He was more of a listener.

Along with everything else going on that Friday morning, the posse's camp was being moved. The original camp was in plain sight of Durand, we found out. He could see everything going on, pretty much keep track of the posse. So the sheriff was moving it out of sight. I headed up to the Owens place to let him know that the radio would be out of operation until the move was done. John Simpson needed to tend the horses corralled there. So we got in my car, and Grandpa Simpson came along. They wanted to go for a spin in my brand-new Buick. I had bought it less than a month ago. It was a beauty.

A mile or so from the camp, I saw a man sitting beside the road, a rifle across his lap. He was wearing blue overalls, a denim jacket and a cap, looking just like I expected a posseman to look. The fellow flagged me down. He pointed to his deputy sheriff's badge, so I knew he was all right. I stopped alongside and rolled down my window. He came up to me and said, "I'm a special deputy assigned to patrol this road. Will you take me into camp?"

It was an ordinary enough request. I hadn't been told that anyone was patrolling the road, but it made sense. The curious would be making their way up here and deputies had been set out to shoo them out of the danger area. So I said, "Sure, hop in." And in he came. "I'm the radio man, Harry Moore, and this guy runs the horses they're using up on the mountain."

The stranger said, "Stop by the creek so I can get my bedroll." I did. He told John Simpson, "Go get my stuff over there." Suddenly he sounded different when he spoke; he was telling John what to do.

John answered bluntly, "You can ask me to get your stuff, but I won't be ordered around in that tone of voice by anyone—and that includes deputy sheriffs. Carry it yourself."

The man shrugged, climbed out and retrieved his bedroll, tossed it into the car, and sat down in the back seat next to Grandpa Simpson. Then he spoke up again; a grim note had crept into his voice. "Turn the car around and drive the other way."

"I can't drive down there," I said. "It doesn't go where I'm heading."

And that's when he said, "No. You're gonna do what I say. I'm the badman they're looking for. I'm Earl Durand." That's the way he put it.

The second I heard that, my defenses went to work. I slammed on the brakes and took the car out of gear. I opened the car door, ready to run back into a clump of trees. In the first moment of fright when somebody threatens you, you're going to react. I leaned out of the car, had one foot on the ground, when the cold iron of his six-shooter pressed against the back of my neck.

"Just stay right where you are and get back in this car," Earl said.

I did what he said. Earl took out two .38 pistols and held them on us from then on. None of the three of us had a weapon. But John wasn't gonna be bested by this character yet. "Why didn't you say who you were before and save all this argument." His half-hearted retort just thumped on the floor.

"Just drive the way I told you," Earl warned us. "You men do as I say and you won't get hurt. I'm sorry I had to kill those two men, but I just had to. You have nothing to be afraid of if you do as I say. Now turn around and head for Powell." There was nothing to do but comply.

When we had gone far enough so no one on the mountain could see us, Earl had me pull off the road and unlock the trunk for him. He stashed his whole arsenal in there except for the two pistols and one rifle. Then he got back in and we took off again.

The three of us had never seen Earl Durand before in our lives. He was supposed to be wild-looking; he sure looked shaggy in the photo the sheriff showed the possemen. This Earl wasn't scruffy. He was the cleanest-looking man up there. I had seen the posse checking through, going on up to hunt for him. Those men coming down, most of them hadn't taken off their clothes since the manhunt began. They hadn't even taken the time to wash their faces or shave their whiskers. They looked a hell of a lot worse than Durand did.

Durand was used to living out in the mountains and taking care of himself. He was still wearing his four-buckle overshoes. It was easy for him to fool me.

IT WAS EIGHT IN THE MORNING and we were forty miles west of Powell. For the next four hours Durand had me drive him all over most of northern Wyoming. The whole time he was nonchalant, off-handed, like we were old acquaintances just bumming around together on a Friday morning. But that wasn't what we were doing at all. We were hostages of a killer making his escape.

The road we were on connected with the Clarks Fork road and went over to Deaver, fifteen miles north of Powell. We took a cutoff, went through some back roads because Durand wanted to stay out of harm's way. They were really just trails, rutted, washboarded, pot-holed, dusty tracks running through ranch land, fields, and pastures and alongside some pretty rugged hills. I got a little sarcastic with Durand. I asked, "Keeping out of harm's way? We're in the thick of harm, not out of its way." Then he said, "If the posse catches up with us, you men just sit still. I'll jump out and fight it out with them so you don't get hurt." I thought to myself, "If something like that gets going, I'm gonna be long gone someplace, I don't know where. Just give me the chance and I'll be gone." Then he ordered, "Go over into the Sand Coulee country and the badlands district. They'll never find us back in there. Fact, I guess they're still looking for me up on the mountain. Now go to Deaver."

I asked Durand, "Where'd you get that deputy's badge?"

"I took it off one of them fellers up on the mountain," Earl said.

He told us about pluggin' Argento and Linabary. He said, "I saw two possemen below me break out of the trees. There was about two hundred feet of clear talus rock between us. I picked the place because no one in his right mind would try to cross the open slope between me and the trees. Those two guys, I could tell they were headed straight for me. There wasn't much I could do. I waited till I knew there was no mistake. Why they were coming on, I'll never know. Did they think I would let them get close enough to shoot me? It was them or me. Bang, bang! I shot one right after the other. I don't think they even knew what hit them."

Durand made no bones about it. Really, those guys had it coming, going up to him like that. What else could he do but shoot?

I told him, "They weren't on the posse, just two independent operators."

"Well, they got operated," Earl said.

I heard some of the guys coming off the posse mention rumors up on the mountain about a pretty chunk of change, a reward for the men who got Earl Durand dead or alive. I figure Linabary or Argento must have got wind of that rumor and said, "You and I will spot him, get him, and split the money between us. Hell, we don't have to split it with those other guys down there." So when they spotted his trail they just thought, "Aha!" They weren't seeing footprints—they just saw dollar signs. They were hunting Earl for the money. In a way you can't feel too sorry for them. Frank Blackburn gave those guys strict orders to stay off the mountain. A sensible man would not disobey an order of Blackburn's, from what I knew of the sheriff. Argento and Linabary didn't live to learn the lesson.

As we drove around, Durand talked about his past day's activities as if he were describing a jaunt to the grocery store. "I followed the posse down from the mountain two nights ago. On the way down, I stopped off and plucked one guy's deputy badge off him. It came in mighty handy, my ticket out. Those guys I shot were carrying a couple of six-shooters each. I took them and ammunition, too. I knew the sheriff would come back with an army and I would be better off someplace else. At the foot of the Beartooths, I turned east and followed along the Littlerock Creek. I circled just below the base camp. I heard the possemen talking, seen them moving about, every one of them buggers carrying a rifle and a six-gun all loaded for me. I bedded down near the creek below the camp. I passed within a hundred feet of them, dang near enough to feel the warmth of their fire. They never knew I was there." He said, "I stayed there the next day and last night. I sure would have liked a fire, but I had to do without. It's mighty cold up there this time of year. I had some food, so I wasn't too hungry." Then Earl asked us, "Say, do you know the names of those two men I killed?" It never occurred to me he didn't know who they were, but then how would he?

I said, "Arthur Argento and some guy name of Linabary."

"I never heard of them," Durand said. Then he went on. "Before sunrise I moved east into a boulder field, thousands of boulders, small ones, mostly, two or three feet high. I picked a comfortable spot to wait for the posse to move out. The posse wasn't looking anywhere near where I was, and even if they had, they'd have never found me. There was just too many boulders to search, and I picked out a spot where I could get up for a look and scoot down in a crevice under two boulders. They'd never know I was there.

"I ran out of food this morning. I decided to go back home where I have friends who'd hide me and feed me. I didn't want to be on the mountain if the sheriff came back today. I got to get out of here as quick as I can."

I wonder who Earl had in mind. He'd sure be putting a strain on friendships by asking for help, and, by that time, I doubt there'd be anyone left who harbored any sympathy for him. But then again, Earl comes charging in asking for food, you by God feed him and no questions asked. Then he said, "I circled around, pretty near got to a car. I'd have taken it, too. A deputy was a little too close though, so I didn't try it."

Durand was planning to steal the sheriff's car until I came along and guaranteed him all the chauffeur service he could use. A few days after this was all over I told Sheriff Blackburn what Earl had said about his car. He answered, "I wouldn't doubt that he would have gotten there before the men." Then he gave one of them Frank Blackburn pauses. I knew he had a remark coming, fit to make a guy burst out laughing. "But I had the key," he said.

Frank Blackburn was one of the last of the old lawmen, the kind you read about in the Westerns. He was professional, practiced his craft for a long time. He was a kind and good man. If he found some kids in trouble, he didn't yank them off to jail. He'd treat them almost like their own fathers would, might wallop their butts and tell them not to let him catch them doing whatever it was they had been doing. And they'd listen to him. A run-in with Sheriff Frank Blackburn of Park County, Wyoming, was something no kid ever relished. His son, Frank, and I used to run around together quite a bit. One time Frank and I got in a squabble on the street at the Mee-teetse barbeque, a big fall celebration. The sheriff come up behind us, grabbed us both by the scruff of the neck and banged us together. He said, "I have enough trouble controlling the drunks without having to put up with you two. Either behave yourselves or get the hell out of town and go home." That's the kind of man he was. And that was his own son.

Earl's conversation was so natural, as if he wanted old acquaintances to know what he had been doing the past few days. It was hard to know exactly what to expect, but at least Durand was calm and civil—you might even say courteous. He never did anything without explaining what he was going to do. The guy didn't seem the least bit crazy. You would never guess he had killed four men, two of them just two days before. He never acted mad or got rough except when he got with his parents. He was never unmannerly with us. Old Mr. Simpson offered Durand a chew of tobacco. "Thank you. I don't use tobacco and I don't drink alcohol," Earl said.

In any case, our job was clear: do whatever Earl said to do. The man was bristling with guns and ammunition. He was a walking arsenal.

You always wonder how you'd act in a fix like this. At the time I wasn't scared. For some reason being scared didn't enter my mind. I started scheming what I could do to get the hell out of the situation. Little things went through my mind. I found myself thinking about Western stories in the drugstore and pool hall book racks. I'm a pretty well-read fella, novels as well as electronics and radio repair books, *Life* magazine, *Mechanix Illustrated*. I guess I was making this into a story to keep it from getting to me. I was thinking about stories I had read, trying to remember a ruse for me and the Simpsons to use to escape. I was thinking very coldly about it, until it was all over and I was home again. As it turned out Earl, let us off without any fuss.

WHEN WE GOT NEAR DEAVER, the gas gauge read empty. I said, "We're out of gas. There's a station in Deaver, but I don't have any money." The Simpsons said they didn't either.

Earl said, "Pull into a station and buy gas. I don't expect you to pay. The ride's on me." He gave me a dollar. As we pulled into the filling station, Earl said, just as calm as you please, "Remember, I

will have the six-shooter at your back. Don't try anything smart."
The mechanic didn't suspect anything.

"Welcome to Deaver," Simpson said, irony in his voice.

Earl ordered me to drive to the train depot. When we stopped, he said, "Lock the doors and give me your keys." He and I went into the express office.

John Simpson told me later that as soon as we were out of the car they began to talk. The younger man said, "Show you how far Durand is out of his element: he doesn't know you can lock a person out of a car, but you can't lock them in. All you have to do is pull up the knob. Durand don't know who we are."

The old man said, "He never asked us our names."

The younger Simpson said, "As far as he's concerned, he no more needs to know who we are than he needs to know the price of tea in China. It would be foolish to try to escape. If you and I try getting away, he might kill Harry. He took Harry along to keep us in the car. Besides, you're not as spry on your feet as you used to be." In fact, old Mr. Simpson walked with a cane and moved pretty slow. "If Earl came back and we weren't here, he'd find us and kill us."

Earl and I went up to the express window. He said to the teller, "I'm Raymond Rayburn. You have a package for me." Earl was using an alias. I'd never heard that name before. The agent went to a bin and came back with a package. Durand signed for the box using the name he had given. He spoke with a couple of other customers. He said, "I'm with the posse. We have Durand trapped. I'll bring back his scalp." He was sure enjoying himself, the role he was playing. We went back to the car. Earl said, "We're going to my folks' house."

On the way, Earl opened his package—ammunition, three hundred rounds of Remington .30–.30 shells. He had enough ammunition and arms to storm a fortress. What did he have planned? We were curious. By now he didn't have any respect for the law. That's what got him in trouble. Still, he could have shot us three any time he wanted to, but he didn't, so he wasn't bloodthirsty, wasn't a wanton killer. As it turned out, he had done all the killing he was gonna do. Our curiosity was up, and so was our fear. This much ammunition in Earl's hands could spell disaster. After parading himself before a posse from a position where they couldn't do anything about him, and then escaping from them altogether, he must have been feeling pretty cocksure of himself. I'll bet he was thinking himself as good as any of the desperadoes he must have admired—the James gang, the Daltons, and the Hole-in-the-Wall criminals. What would he do if he ran into a situation where he had to kill a lot of people? There was no question in my mind that he wouldn't hesitate. I just hoped we weren't "in that number."

When we got closer to his folk's farm, Durand said, "Drive careful. Someone might be laying in wait. Be ready to throw the car in reverse and give it the gas if I tell you."

THE GUY WAS NO HERO. The scene with Earl and his folks—if I had any compassion left for him, I lost it then. I drove in slowly so Earl could take a look around. His father was outside carrying equipment to the barn.

Earl rolled down his window and called out, "Surprised to see me, Dad?"

Mr. Durand turned to face us. His lips tightened into a grim line. He didn't speak.

With anger in his voice sharp as a knife edge, Earl said, "Come over here."

Mr. Durand started walking slowly toward the car. Earl said, "I want some things, Dad. Do you give them to me or do I have to get them with a gun?"

His father shook his head. "Get what you want, Earl."

With his rifle under one arm and a six-shooter in the other hand, Earl got out and walked his father off in the direction of his tent. They were out of earshot. Earl had spoken to us in a civil tone. I couldn't make out exactly what Earl was saying, but I could tell that old Mr. Durand was being berated, scolded, ordered around. Earl jabbed the old man's shoulder with his finger. I couldn't tell whether Mr. Durand was backing away from Earl or whether Earl was pushing him.

I've often wondered what Earl said. Was he blaming his family for what happened? Did he expect them to help him out of his predicament? I don't think so. By this time everything was matter-of-fact for

Earl. In the Western story magazines I read, people don't do things for a reason. The characters are just the way they are and do what they do. You only see one side of the character, the side that fits the story. They never tell you that at the age of twelve the bad guy felt the Holy Spirit move in him, confessed his sins, was baptized, and believes to this day that he will go to hell for his abominable sins. Or maybe another villain as a kid built a crystal radio set and listened night after night, fascinated by the world opening before him. They don't write that in the Western magazines because the stories of bad guys, good guys, and exciting plots have no reason to explain a villain. You've got to show him rotten and show him being rotten. Matter-of-fact as a Western story—that's how Earl must have talked to his father.

After Earl finished, old Mr. Durand, broken-spirited, just turned and walked away. I said to myself, "The old man's just given up."

Then Earl came and got me, forced me to walk ahead of him toward his tent, too. He said, "Hurry up." He went inside and handed me out a small sack of salt and a bigger one with cornmeal in it. We headed back to the car. His mother came running from the house. "Oh Earl," she sobbed, "I hardly know you!"

His mother, like all mothers would be, was brokenhearted. Over and over she moaned, "Oh, Earl. Oh, Earl," and tears were streaming down her face. But instead of walking over to her and being kind to his old mother—which would have made me think the kid's still got some good in him—Earl smart-alecked her.

"I just came back to say hello. I've got more important stuff to do than listen to your crying." That's what he said to his mother.

"What do you mean, Earl?" his mother asked, her voice choked up with sobbing.

Earl didn't answer, just hurried over to the car and got in.

Heartbroken and distraught, his parents were stunned. All the hopes a parent has for a child were dashed, and in their place was despair and shame. Filled with compassion for the couple, I walked slowly past Mr. Durand. He turned to me and said, "Sir, I don't even know who you three men are. But I want you to know this certainly is a surprise to us, and a terrible blow. We are sorry for what our son has done."

"I know, Mr. Durand. We're all sorry," was all I could muster.

I got back into the car slowly. Earl overheard his father's words, but all he said was, "Drive." As the car pulled out of the yard, Durand shouted back to his parents, like he was suddenly off on a joy ride, "I'll be seeing you, Dad!" Those were the last words his poor folks heard. Just that stupid "I'll be seeing you!" Even as he spoke, his thoughts must have been somewhere else. He knew dang well he wasn't going to see them again.

Earl had me drive up to an abandoned coal mine three miles north of the family place. The mine was up on a hill and out of sight of the road. He said, "Get out. This is as far as you go." I thought he meant that this was where he was going to finish us off. Instead, we got out and he smashed out the wing windows of my brand-new car with the butt end of a pistol. "If I have to shoot, I don't want to get cut with glass from my own bullets," he said. He asked me, in a joking way, "Do you have theft and damage insurance on this car?" I did. "Then you'll be able to collect on your car. Just tell them that Earl Durand is to blame." He laughed.

Then he pointed to a house down below in a windbreak of trees. "That house has a telephone. Tell them I sent you. They'll give you a ride into town. After I get out of sight, why, you can take off." He wasn't concerned that we'd get out of there too quick.

Earl stalled the car, then started it again. He shouted out the broken ventilator window to us, "Be sure and come to my funeral!" and honked the horn. With that crack I knew the end of this story hadn't been wrote yet. There was more to come.

He put the car in first, ground the gears, and jerked on down the trail, just like I expected.

The three of us talked a little as we walked the half-hour to the house, old man Simpson slowing us down some. Simpson asked, "Where do you think he'll go? If he can get across Montana, he can cross the border to Canada. Now there's a place to hide."

Thinking about my car, I said, "I don't think he can get very far on a dollar's worth of gas. He'll need more money."

Simpson said, "I think we came close to being killed."

Grandpa Simpson spoke up for the second time the whole four-hour trip: "It's a miracle we're still alive."

"I've had more excitement than I ever wanted," I said. "I'll take adventure in the magazines and the movies. I don't crave any more of the real thing."

It took a few minutes of knocking at the door to rouse the lady inside. We told her what had happened and asked if we could use her telephone. I couldn't reach any law officers but finally found the city clerk. I told him, "Earl Durand just took my car and is probably on his way into town. Be on the lookout for him."

He said, "Well, don't worry. He already arrived at the bank and we just killed him."

I said, "Well, I wasn't particularly worried. I just wanted to let you know. I didn't know whether he'd gone there or not. He didn't tell us his plans when he left us."

Durand hadn't told us he was going to rob the bank, but I think when he dumped us he knew what he was going to do. The idea must have occurred to him while we were driving around. Not only would he need money for gas and food, I understand he had hard feelings for R. A. Nelson at the bank. Right or wrong, very few bankers were loved at that time anyhow. I think that's why he blew out all the bank's windows. Later I heard he had a habit of just holding the trigger down and pumping the rifle. It was something he knew about guns. That's probably what he did in the bank.

When I heard about all the gunfire inside and outside the bank, I was surprised more folks weren't hit. There were a lot of people shooting when the men came out of the bank. As soon as John Gawthrop stepped out the bank door, some trigger-happy fools let loose, figuring that the first person out the door would be the bandit. It wasn't.

The family at the farm drove us into town and dropped us off right near the bank. The town was packed. There were traffic jams on the streets, something brand new to Powell. You'd think it was the carnival or circus in town.

I wanted to get in my car and just drive home, but the car couldn't be found. I asked and asked, and finally someone told me about a car that fit the description I gave. It was used to drive Johnny Gawthrop to the hospital. I knew the kid, just as nice a young fella as you'd ever want to meet. I hitched a ride with a law officer. The car was parked in the driveway, the keys still in the ignition. There was John's blood all over the back seat. The deputy and I spent the next hour down at the gas station hosing the blood off and giving my back seat a hell of a soaking. It took days to dry out.

EARL LET US LIVE, NEVER made an issue about it at all, never a fuss about anything. With us he was still being Earl the good neighbor.

What I got a kick out of was that Earl took my car knowing nobody expected to see him come driving into town. If he walked down the street he'd have been recognized. That's how he got clear down to the middle of town without anybody knowing it was him.

I came to the conclusion that Durand realized that, all right, he had killed four people. Then he was thinking he was gonna go out in a blaze of glory. He didn't even want to get out of the jam. There was no reason for him to go in the bank and shoot it up. He could have gotten the money and got out of there and been long gone before anybody outside the bank knew he had been there.

The thing that threw Earl, he shifted from the ways he knew to the modern ways, and he got nailed. In other words, in the car and the bank he tried to be a modern desperado. On horse or on foot he couldn't be beat. He could range clear down into Mexico or up into Canada, following the Rocky Mountains. He could live off the land. He had no problem there. His salt and meal was all he needed. But he was no good at robbing a bank.

I WAS BUSHED, FELT LIKE I had spent a lifetime in that car with Earl Durand instead of only four hours. I couldn't stop thinking about the day's events. It so happened that when I finally got home, a friend of mine, a nurse, was at the house. She handed me a couple of pills and said, "You'd better take these, Harry."

I said, "I'm just pooped. I don't need anything. I feel just fine."

"No, you'd better take these before you lie down."

"Oh, I don't need anything. I feel fine."

Finally she said, "Take them. Do what I tell you." You know how nurses are.

I took the pills and lay down. Just as I was relaxing, everything that had been holding me together fell apart. I started going to pieces. I thought what could have happened. Suddenly it all caught up with me. About that time the pills worked. I could see why she wanted me to take them. She knew there was going to be a letdown, a lot of fear, and I'd better be out of it when it hit. I was scared and shaky all at once. The pills worked. Everything was fine then.

I gave a telephone interview to a reporter on the *Denver Post*. I was the last person to have a friendly conversation with Earl Durand. The story appeared in the newspaper just the way I had told it and I got a by-line—"As reported by Harry Moore."

The next day I took the car into the agency where I had bought it the month before. Fortunately they had a couple of wing windows in stock. The repairman—I knew him from town pretty well—he worked till noon on Saturdays. It didn't take him long to install those windows, and I was on my way like nothing had ever happened.

THE

BANK ROBBERY

The exuberance of a maniac finally burst in him. Laughing, shouting, cursing, he shot up the inside of the bank, then shot out the windows and into the shop windows along Main Street.

Cody Enterprise, March 29

THREE SHOTS FIRED IN WILD GUN BATTLE
ENDS TARZAN'S BLOODY REIGN

It was consistent with his bravado that he chose the reckless, dramatic denouement of a bank robbery, knowing, as he had said in a note to the sheriff, that he was "done for."

Denver Post, March 25

Vastalee Dutton

Bank Customer

JIMMY AND I OWNED the Ralston service station and mechanic garage. Back then Mr. Durand, Earl's father, owned a school bus service. Jimmy and his mechanics kept the buses in running order. About the time Earl quit school, he started driving the school bus mornings and afternoons. Jimmy knew the family and Earl quite well, but I didn't know Earl hardly at all. I once saw him at the station. He wore his hair cut off square down below his shoulders. He was clean-shaven, being still a boy. He wore blue jeans and a blue chambray shirt. He was striding along, a big angular fellow. A woman notices looks and dress. Then I didn't see him again for years—until I caught a glimpse of him up at Beartooth Mountain. Yes, I did!

Then, of course, at the bank.

For many years before Earl's last days the word was about that he lived in the open country, taking food from ranches and sheep camps and killing wild game without a license or any care for the law. I don't know about that for certain; it's just what I heard.

The autumn before Earl's rampage Jimmy's hunting dog once led him down a faint path to a shelter on our ranch on the Lower Bench. The shelter was built in the center of a thicket. It was scrub branches woven together. Jimmy said Earl Durand must have built it.

I didn't know anything about Earl being arrested until a car sales-man stopped by our station and told me that Earl Durand was in jail in Cody. He said to me, "I have one hundred dollars to bet that Earl will break jail. He would hate to be inside four walls." Of course, I wouldn't bet on such a thing.

JIMMY WAS A WIDOWER when I met him. His daughter, Virginia, was married to Don Wright. When the troubles came up with Earl, Frank Blackburn swore in both Jimmy and Don for the posse. Father-in-law and son-in-law. They were also good friends, hunting buddies, both members of the Heart Mountain Gun Club and the Masonic Lodge. They enjoyed each other's company. We were a happy family. Virginia and Don had a year-old boy named Jimmy after his granddad.

Virginia was distraught over everything that was happening. That Friday at about seven in the morning, I took her up to the Owens ranch so she could visit Don, but he wasn't around. We visited for a while with the men we knew on the posse, passing the time. I took some pictures of the area. Finally we had to leave. Virginia did not get to see her husband. As we were driving off I saw someone running from one tree to another over towards an old corral the posse was using. I said, "That's Earl Durand. Over there by the corral, it's Earl. I see him!" Of course Virginia and the few possemen thought I was out of my mind, but it turned out that I was right. It was Earl on his way out.

I dropped Virginia off and went home and did some housework. Then I ate lunch and went into Powell to help my mother with her banking. Mother had a check she wanted to deposit. The First National Bank faces south on Main Street. There are tall windows along the sidewalk on the west side. When you walk in, on the right starts a wood railing about hip-high with a gate passing through. The officers had their desks behind the railing. After the railing the tellers' cages begin, with a marble front and brass grillwork going up higher than your head. The vault where the safe deposit boxes were was at the back end of the building.

Mother and I were at the first teller's cage and Edgar Swallow was waiting on her. Of course we knew Edgar from way back. He was an elderly gentleman. Mother had just endorsed the check and slipped it through the grill to Edgar.

It all happened very quickly. I heard rattle, rattle, rattle. I looked up and toward the door. A man was running into the bank. He had a shoulder-strap satchel made of canvas, like an old-fashioned school

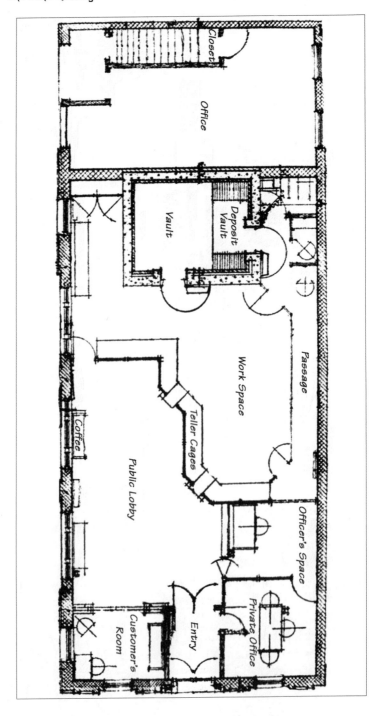

Interior, First National Bank of Powell. Adapted from a blueprint provided by the First National Bank of Powell.

satchel. It was full of shells and they were rattling. He carried a .30–.30 rifle. Well, everyone was carrying a rifle in town since Durand had killed the town marshal and the deputy sheriff, but then I recognized the man as Earl. He spun around and shouted, "This is a holdup! Put your hands up in the air!" And he fired.

It was so loud I thought a bomb had exploded. After that I couldn't hear anything. After that first shot I looked at Edgar. His face drained white. Earl shot over our heads. The bullet went through a feathered decoration shaped like a bird's wing on my hat. I had bought it to wear for Easter. The hat took a dive off of my head. I was so scared I didn't notice at the time—I found it later.

Then Earl shouted, "Everybody line up against the wall and keep your hands in the air." Terrified, we all did what he said. There were four other customers in the bank besides my mother, Mrs. Laura Dooley, and me: there was Harry Hecht, from the lumber-yard, our dentist, Dr. J. C. Stahn, and Dan Fritz from Cody. There was E. P. Guenther. My mother, bless her heart, couldn't hold her hands way up in the sky like I did—mine were stretched clear to the ceiling. She put her elbows on the thick glass-topped counter to support her hands.

Earl ordered the bank employees to open the vault. They told him they could get extra money from a small vault where some extra cash is held. Durand told Maury Knutson to open it up. He kept his rifle weaving back and forth between Maury and the rest of us the whole time. Maury got the box out. He begged Durand, "Please, don't shoot me." I can still hear the quiver in his voice. "Please don't shoot me." Maury was scared because Earl was shooting all the time, shooting out the windows on the west side of the building. He made us face the wall, not even glance to the side. The rest of us were absolutely silent, dumbfounded. We were paralyzed, afraid we might draw the next bullet. But they say I was praying at the top of my lungs.

I don't remember anything about it. I was really in shock, I can tell you, in a fog. I saw pictures of places and events from my life long ago. I sat beside a stream flowing full in springtime, listening to water rippling over the stones, watching swirls and dips as the water passed on its way. I saw wildflowers in bloom, heard the caws of a flock of magpies settling in the cottonwood trees. For a time, this motion picture was more real to me than Earl shooting and shouting, more real than the wall I was facing, than our bobbing up and down like wind-up toys to the beat of the gunshots. My mind couldn't stand to be where it really was and picked out a safe place to visit while the horror was unfolding. Then I started seeing imaginary horrors. I saw all of us dead on the floor, blood splattered all over the walls, running down, and the floor looking like a slaughterhouse. Then I saw a picture of Earl hitting a beef cow over the head with a sledgehammer. Finally, my thoughts returned to reality and I could see I wasn't thinking right.

After Durand got all the money, he was ready to leave. I knew something was going to happen because he shouted, "You! And you! And you! Get over here!" Edgar Swallow was standing next to me. He turned and walked toward Earl. Durand said, "Get back. I got all the guys I want." Earl tied up young Johnny Gawthrop, Maury, and R.A. Nelson. I watched them leave the bank, Earl prodding them forward and holding them back at the same time with a cord or rope.

Suddenly there were more gunshots. Earl rushed back into the bank and fell down just inside the door to the left. By sheer willpower, Earl got a hold of his holster pistol. His hand was shaking, his arm, too. He rubbed the point of the pistol against his neck and managed to pull the trigger. My God! I covered my face with my hands and screamed. I had never seen a man shoot himself before. When Mr. Nelson got his hands untied, he heard shots inside and thought Earl was killing us. He grabbed Durand's rifle off the sidewalk, came in, and shot Earl in the head from only a few inches away. Oh, the blood.

I had taken Mother's hand and forced her to lie down on the floor, where we stayed until things quieted down. Under unusual strain we do the oddest things. While I lay there I was picking up empty cartridges from Earl's rifle, if you can imagine that.

WHEN THE SHOOTING FINALLY stopped, a man I didn't know came running into the bank. He had a hunting knife in his hand. I had this bizarre notion that he was going to scalp Earl. Where I ever got such a crazy idea, I'll never know. I must have been ready for anything savage or cruel. But the man took his knife and cut the canvas strap on the satchel in two while it was still slung over Earl's shoulder. He handed the satchel over to one of the bank employees. It was crammed full of money and ammunition.

They say Durand had fired forty or fifty rounds. Earl shot out the windows. I was told he was shooting high. Outside, the bullets had gone everywhere, hitting all over the place. Bullets went into the Wyoming Hotel; one whizzed by the cage of a canary bird that used to sing so beautiful. After that it just sat in its cage, flew around the way it used to, but it didn't even peep till the next week. Another bullet hit a moose head mounted in the lobby right between the eyes. Earl couldn't have done better if the moose had been his target. Bullets smacked through the walls of guests' rooms. One bullet went into the back of a car. D. M. Baker had a real estate office in town. It had a little sign over the door. A bullet went through that sign, went right through the "k" in his name. It wasn't enough that Earl had killed the man, now his bullets were wrecking his sign. I had driven my mother's car from her house to the bank and parked on the west side of the bank. The license plate stuck out a little past the fender; a bullet went right through the plate and missed the car. These were like strange feats of marksmanship.

Naturally, the first thing I intended to do was to drive Mother home and get her settled in. I helped her get to her feet. But I was in complete shock. Driving away from the bank, instead of going west and heading for the Powell highway, I turned right and went east. I just wanted to get away from that place. I didn't know where I was going, what I was doing. You do some very odd things when you're in shock.

Jimmy came into town with the rest of the posse. Someone told him that I had been in the bank. First thing, he called the doctor and asked him if he had seen me. When the doctor said no, Jimmy told him to go to the house and see how I was doing. The doctor gave me a sedative that knocked me out and stopped the horrible headache that had come on.

After I rested overnight I was all right. The next morning—Saturday it was—I took Mother back to the bank to see about her check. We got there just as it was opening. Nothing had been touched from the day before. Edgar picked up Mother's check from the floor. He showed us where the first bullet had struck the wall near the vault. "Vastalee, you were standing directly in the line of fire," Edgar said. "I don't know how you're still alive today."

I said, "Well, neither do I. You know, my hat flew off my head and I didn't even realize it till just now. There it is, over there on the floor." I picked up my new Easter hat, set it on my head, then took it off. The three of us looked at it. It didn't look right. Then I discovered a bullet hole right through the feathered decoration. The bullet missed my scalp by an inch, no more. Of course, Durand didn't mean to kill me, but if he had, it wouldn't have made any difference to him. He wouldn't have even stopped to say, "Excuse me." If I had been standing one step forward, I would have been dead.

Then Edgar deposited Mother's check and we left.

LATER THAT DAY THE HUNTER and guide from Greybull, Bob White, stopped by the service station. He had heard about my hat. He offered me one hundred dollars for it. He wanted to take the hat to the San Francisco World's Fair, put it on display, and sell tickets to the fairgoers to see it. He also offered fifty dollars for my mother's license plate with the bullet hole through it, and he had his eye on the canary in its damaged cage from the Wyoming Hotel. But my husband said, "We are not going to use the misfortune of many people to profit for ourselves." He wasn't the only one who tried to cash in on the events. A car dealer in Denver ran a big ad in the *Denver Post*. "TARZAN'S CORNERED," it said, and "So Have We Cornered All the Finest Used Cars in the West."

The next Labor Day weekend Jimmy and I went to Thermopolis to the rodeo—a big annual event. Milward Simpson was master of ceremonies that year. My husband and I were making all the fun places. In the evening we went into a bar with another couple. It was a big place; inside were three columns. I happened to look up and saw a death mask at the top of each column. I said, "Jimmy, that's Earl Durand up there!"

He looked up and saw the masks. "Oh, you're out of your mind. You haven't had anything to drink yet, so I know you're sober. That can't be Durand."

A man came over and said, "I beg your pardon, but I couldn't help but overhear. The lady is right. Bob White made these. He was in Powell when Durand was killed and made a plaster cast of his face. He made several masks, and here they hang." White hadn't told us about the mask when he tried to buy my hat. He must have intended it as the centerpiece of his exhibit at the fair. But that never came off.

White is the taxidermist who mounted the two-thousand-pound buffalo on display in the rotunda of the state capitol in Cheyenne. I went right to see him at his shop in Thermopolis. He told me, "I have a home up in Greybull. I have the plaster cast of Durand's face stored up in the attic. Next time I'm up in the attic I'll bring the form down and make you a mask." Eventually he did. But it took him a long time. It was after fifteen years of asking him that he finally made it for me. He did a very good job. It is just like Earl.

So I had another souvenir of the day when I saw Earl twice, morning and afternoon, living and dead.

Maurice Knutson

Bank Cashier

WHEN SHERIFF BLACKBURN viewed Earl Durand's bloody
corpse at Powell Mortuary, he recalled the return address
the desperado had written on the taunting note to
him, Earl Durand, Undertaker's office, Powell, Wyo.
Official Detective, July 1939

ON THE FIRST EVENING OF Durand's rampage, long before I became
involved in half an hour of terror and desperation, I had just come
home from the bank when the telephone rang. I answered. "This is a
line call," the operator said. "I repeat, this is a line call. Earl Durand
has escaped from Cody Jail. He is believed to be armed and is considered dangerous. Lock your house; lock your doors." There was no
alarm in her voice. She spoke in the tone operators are trained to use:
firm, clear, definite. Then she repeated the message. In those days the
local phone company could ring all the telephones in the system and
talk to everyone all at once. Usually they announced school closings
due to snow and that was about it. I don't remember them ever using
it for emergencies before or after. Within an hour of that call Durand
had killed my friends D. M. Baker and Chuck Lewis.

With that, and Durand's disappearance, the community became
a tense, uncomfortable place to live. Folks didn't sleep well; they
were nervous. The deaths struck us as a terrible tragedy. There was a
feeling of deep depression. No one knew what was going to happen
next, where Durand would next appear. Everyone in town was glued
to the radio for bulletins. When the pursuit for the killer of two law
officers began, the story was national news.

Durand showed up at several homes right after the killings, scared folks near to death with his guns and his crazy talk. Earl was a local boy many people knew; they found it impossible to believe that he was acting this way.

My first meeting with Earl took place long before these events. One day a man entered the bank. He had long hair and a beard. I was startled by his looks. He presented me with a check from a hide and fur buyer. I didn't ask him for identification; the check wasn't for much money. As he was leaving I whispered to Edgar Swallow, "Who's that?" "That's Earl Durand." As Durand was walking out I noticed he wore moccasins and buckskin trousers and had a hunting knife strapped to his belt. I later heard about his prowess with a knife. He could do wonders throwing a knife. Some kids used to go with him into the hills. One told me that he saw Earl throw his knife at a snake and kill it. The next time I saw him was at a little skating party out at the gravel pit. In winter the pond there was a local recreation area. It was a terribly cold night; everyone was standing around a bonfire trying to warm up, and here was this fellow, his shirt open, skating madly all by himself, a good skater.

WE STARTED WORK AT THE bank at nine. On what was to be Earl's last day, I greeted Johnny Gawthrop and asked, "How are you feeling? How did you sleep?"

He said, "I had a miserable night. I just couldn't sleep."

"Me, too. What do you think is going to happen?"

"I imagined that Earl Durand would come in the bank. I just hope he doesn't," he said.

"There's no chance of that!" I said with great confidence to discount Johnny's offhand remark.

Bob Nelson told us, "The *Billings Gazette* set up a fund for the families of the four men Durand killed—the Wyoming Heroes Fund."

"From what I've heard I'm not so sure those last two are heroes," I said, referring to Linabary and Argento.

Then it was one in the afternoon; we were all back from lunch.

Johnny said, "Friday afternoon. Who's the poor guy working tomorrow?"

I said, "Must be Edgar, 'cause it's not me."

There were the usual "poor sucker!" remarks and jibes back from him. I said to old Mr. Swallow, "I'll think about you when I'm up in the mountains."

"Think all you want, Knutson," he said. "You'll be here next Saturday and I'll be on the river with my fly rod."

Nine of us were in the bank: Bob Nelson, who was the president, three employees, and five customers. The few customers were taken care of. It was quiet. Then there was a disturbance at the door and suddenly a shot rang out, sounding like a cannon going off in the bank. It hit the vault. I was standing near it. Incredible as it seemed, there was Earl Durand, yelling and screaming. He ordered us to line up against the east wall of the lobby, then started shooting out the windows. I was closest to him. Each time he fired, we bobbed up and down, just like we were doing calisthenics. The man standing next to me had extremely bowed legs. I noticed that his knees were knocking and I couldn't figure out how that could be. With each shot I thought he was shooting at the people in line. I thought he started at the farthest from me and was working his way down. I was so frightened, I didn't even turn my head to look. And all the while Durand yelled and screamed.

The tellers' cages were easy to get at from the front, even though they had high steel grills and only a small space to pass money and documents through. Earl reached in all three openings, rifled the tills and stuffed money into a sack he was carrying. Every one of us was in terror, figuring he was going to kill us. Facing the wall, we couldn't see what was happening. I lost all track of time. I couldn't tell how long there was between shots, how many shots were fired. Later the newspapers reported that he fired off forty or fifty rounds. But who knows how the reporter knew or how accurate he was? Sometimes it seemed to me like I had spent most of my life standing in that one spot, calmly listening to the horrendous explosions. Other moments my mind was completely blank, empty, as if I didn't ever exist, never had.

Earl rushed over and picked me. "You, get me more money!" He stood about five feet away from me, waving his gun back and forth. Every time it came to me, it pointed right at my chest. People used silver dollars a lot. I began to haul out bags of silver dollars, not thinking a thing about it. I'd have hauled until there wasn't a bag left, moving on to half-dollars, quarters, dimes, nickels, pennies—until Durand was satisfied. After I brought out two bags, Earl shouted, "That's enough! I don't want any more. It's too heavy. I want more money! You got money in there!" He meant bills. I said, "I can't get you any more because the safe is time-locked."

Durand didn't understand what I was talking about, and, like the safe, my brain was locked. I couldn't think of a word to say, a way to explain the problem so Earl would understand. "You're lying! Open the damn safe!" My brain was just as solid as the door of the steel vault, not a thought moving in it. I knew the lock's combination and I got it the first time. The tumblers clicked, but it didn't make the least bit of difference, because the time lock overrode the tumblers. The lock was set to a timer. Until the clock said so, there was nothing you could do to open it. There I was, acting like Earl's desire for the money and my fear for my life might make a difference. Then I tried to explain to Earl a second time. I said, "The safe won't open because the time lock overrides the tumblers. The safe is time-locked."

Unsympathetic, Earl stood in the vault vestibule, pointing his rifle at my chest. He swung it away and up toward the windows and fired another round, shouting, "You're lying! You're lying! I ought to kill you for this. Open that safe or I'll kill you!" With every passing second I knew my chances of getting out alive were growing slimmer and slimmer. My brain and my body stopped working. The world was fading into deeper and deeper blackness. The climax was coming and I was going to faint and die before I could see how this was going to end. I was at my wits' end, when just five minutes ago I had been wisecracking about poor Edgar Swallow having to work on Saturday while the rest of us would be enjoying a carefree weekend. The injustice of it, the horror of it, overwhelmed me. I would have broken down and cried in my misery and sorrow. Oh, what had I done to deserve this, I asked myself, filled with self-pity. From empty-headedness one second to torrents of uncontrollable thought the next. I hadn't realized the mind and the emotions were capable of such sudden, drastic swings. Then in dumbfounded silence I watched Durand's finger tighten on the trigger while the gun was pointed at me. My eyes brimmed with tears; my throat swelled. I was suffocating, choking on my hopelessness. I saw little chance of getting out of this. There was no possibility. My wife and I had quarreled during lunch that day. I wanted so much to tell her that it was all right and that I was not angry. But I couldn't call anyone, couldn't write a note, couldn't do anything except look at Durand with his gun pointed at me.

Just as Durand was about to trip the trigger, Johnny Gawthrop, teller and bookkeeper, spoke up in the calmest voice. "There is no way you can get any money because I locked the safe. I set the timer and it won't open until three o'clock."

Then Nelson said, "Earl, none of us can open the vault now, not even if you kill us all."

That did it. Broke the spell.

Durand shouted, "I still want more money!"

I don't know why I hadn't thought of it before, but alongside the main vault was a small vault where we kept a safe-deposit box containing two or three thousand dollars in reserve in case there were unusual withdrawals. When I remembered that, I told Earl, "We have some money I can get you out of the other vault." It had a regular vault door. The two vaults were separated inside by an iron grill. You could see through one to the other.

The whole time I had worked at the bank, I had never been able to open the door to this vault on the first try, its lock was so fine, and the numbers had to be centered so precisely on the marker. In fact, my bitter complaints about it were a regular source of amusement among the rest of the staff. "We've got to do something about this lock," I'd say, and they'd sputter and laugh, smirk and smile, offer a few humorous words, no harm intended. "I'm spending all my time getting this danged door open for customers." And here I was, needing to open the door in one heck of a hurry, my life, and the lives of all of us hanging in the balance. I was sure this moment had a special meaning to the other bank employees who were watching: their comeuppance, all the jokes about my thick fingers and unsteady grasp turning to the taste of brass on their tongues, coming back to haunt them like bad jokes have a way of doing. I was even less likely to open the lock now, under the strain and my own nervous shaking. If I failed now, I was afraid Durand's patience would run out.

He was still yelling, now screaming, "I won't get out of this alive! The money isn't going to do me any good!" I could hear our doom in his frustration. "It doesn't matter. I likely won't get out alive to use it anyhow." I felt my gorge rising, breathed deeply to hold my stomach down. Suddenly my head was throbbing with a pounding headache. It felt like my brain was going to explode. Earl followed me with his rifle poking my back. There was an employees' bathroom right next to the vault. For an instant I thought, I'm going to duck in there. I was looking for any way out. But the gun was at my back, and there it stayed while I worked on the combination. I managed to open the vault on the first try for the first time in the entire history of my employ with the bank. I opened the safe-deposit box and gave him all the money. It must have come to about two thousand dollars, surely enough to get him whatever he wanted. That satisfied him. He said, "Get back in the line." I was rescued from death.

Now Earl moved from the vault to the tellers' cages. "This gun barrel is getting too hot to hold." He also put two six-shooters on the counter, one on each side of him. "I need three of you," ordered Earl. "You! You! And you! Get over here!" Edgar Swallow thought Earl had pointed to him, but Earl said, "I don't want you." He knew Edgar, an old-timer.

I was the first one he called out of the line. Earl went over to the teller's side of the cage. "Put your hands through the cage," he said. I could barely get my hands through. He tied them together with a rawhide thong, tied them tight. "Stand right next to this cage," he said to me. Then he motioned Johnny Gawthrop forward and Bob Nelson, had them stick their hands under the grill and tied them, too, both hands together. We found out later that he tied Bob with the leather laces from the boot of one of the fellows he killed up on the mountain. That was horrible—eerie. I don't know what knot he used, but straining at it didn't do any good. It stayed tight no matter what I did. Johnny stood to my right, Bob to my left. Then he came around to the lobby and tied the three of us together with a long rope. He put the rope between our wrists and tied it tight. The whole time he continued shooting and shouting. Durand dragged us to the door like a bunch of mules, then got behind and pushed us out. He was using us as a shield to get himself to the car so he could make his escape. Because the door was so narrow, we could only go out one at a time. Durand pushed Gawthrop out in front, I was in the middle, and Nelson brought up the rear.

Outside at the back of the building, steps led up to the roof. Some men had climbed up when the shooting started inside. Everyone in town was carrying rifles. Just as I stepped out of the door, two shots came from atop the bank, the bullets hitting between Durand and me. We were two feet apart. Concrete shards flew from the sidewalk. Had I stepped down onto the sidewalk, I would have been dead. When Johnny Gawthrop stepped onto it, shots came from down the street, and he fell. Then Nelson fell, pulled down by Gawthrop, pulling me down, too. I crawled behind the front door to get what cover I could—it was a heavy door, with glass and a copper kick plate. My hands stuck out into the street because they were tied to Johnny Gawthrop.

Just as I got behind the door, someone fired a shotgun and hit Johnny again. The poor boy was hit twice. Johnny said, "Thank God it was me and not one of you two married fellows." Then he lost consciousness. I got a little bit of slack because Earl let go of the thong. He was firing wildly in every direction. I tried to get back inside the bank. Earl lunged past me; he had been shot, too. He staggered and fell inside the door two or three feet away from me, took out one of his six-shooters. I was facing out of the bank so I couldn't see what he did next. I heard his gun go off. What was he shooting at? It turns out he shot himself in the neck.

Bob got loose from the rope and rawhide, grabbed Durand's rifle, rushed in, and shot him in the head. He didn't seem to know if Durand was alive or dead. It looked like he wasn't taking any chances. Somebody let fly a shot, even with a big crowd quickly gathering, and a brick fell down from atop the bank. I shouted, "Stop, you idiot! What the hell's the matter with you, you damn fool!" Another fellow just shot in the general direction of the bank. There was all this shooting going on, so he joined in. Everyone wanted to get in on the act. It was that kind of a thing. I had untied myself and turned to see what I could do for Johnny Gawthrop. I got down and listened to Johnny's heart and said, "His heart is still beating! Get a car." I was beside myself. Some people got him into a car and drove him off to the hospital. He died just as he got there.

I needed to let my wife know I was alive. I called her on the phone. When she answered I said, "Hello, Jane. Maury. I'm okay. I don't know if you've heard what happened here at the bank. I'll tell you later."

"You're alive!" she cried. "The holdup was broadcast on the radio. We heard the gunshots. A news bulletin announced that you were killed. We heard the gunshots. The radio reported you were dead. Oh, God, is it really you? You'd better send a telegram to your folks."

"I love you," I said. I sent a night wire to my folks back in Wisconsin where I was from. It's a good thing I did. When I talked to my mother and father on the phone the next day, they told me they heard I had been killed. I told them that a miracle had happened. There was no reason I should have been alive, and I've felt that way ever since.

ALL THAT NIGHT I TOSSED and couldn't sleep. I had been through a terrible trauma. It's amazing to think how much of your life can take place in twenty minutes.

If you can imagine the mess in the bank—every window shot out, money scattered all over and mixed in with broken glass. I was the one who had to clean the place up.

Monday Johnny was buried. The bank was closed out of respect for him. We all went to the funeral. All the stores in town closed for the time of his funeral. The church was full. Many stood outside in a cold wind and driving snow. The funeral cortege stretched more than a mile on the way to the Riverside Cemetery.

For weeks I couldn't sleep at night. Bob Nelson was unable to work at all. Johnny was dead. It was the most horrible summer I ever spent. About a year later I went into ranching. Banking was too dangerous.

At the time I was young and fairly good-looking. One of the movie studios offered to bring me to Hollywood for a screen test. They were trying to capitalize on the story. They probably had a press agent at work painting the picture in words: "See the movie with the man who faced down the 'Tarzan of the Tetons.'" I wouldn't be surprised if they were planning a movie about the story. But I refused. I just wanted to forget all about "Tarzan" and my rescue from death. Besides, I had no desire to become a Hollywood actor.

Pathe News featured the Durand affair in its newsreel for the week. When it played in my hometown in Wisconsin, the theater owner advertised it with a come-on: "Local Boy Victim of Durand Hold-Up. See Knutson Show How He Escaped with His Life." I heard it brought in big crowds.

The newsreel also played at the Teton Theatre in Cody. People around here were sick of the story and didn't go out of their way to see it. My interest in history and in the making of history—plus my own involvement in the events—prompted me to attend. Aside from the time when Durand was actually in the bank, seeing the Pathe newsreel was as odd an experience as I've ever had. There was footage of the manhunt out in the Beartooth Mountains, of the bank, with a dramatization of what happened there featuring me, Bob Nelson, and Edgar Swallow standing in for Johnny Gawthrop. Tip Cox "shot" Durand again for the camera.

But for some strange reason, the newsreel scene that stuck in my mind was the interview with Mrs. Bill Monday. She stood in front of Bill's airplane parked on the meadow, the Beartooth Mountains in the background.

Announcer: *"Trailing a killer by airplane is a unique way to spend a honeymoon. Mr. and Mrs. Bill Monday were just married and are finding life plenty exciting. Monday, a Cody, Wyoming, official, is liaison officer for the forces seeking to capture Earl Durand. Mrs. Monday has been with him on all of his dangerous flights."*

Mrs. Monday: *"I expected being married to Bill would lead to a life of excitement. But I've already had enough excitement to last a lifetime. One day I ride on a seat filled with explosives, and the next I sit next to armed men who are hunting Earl Durand. Both Bill and I have gone without sleep for more than thirty hours."*

I've forgotten what movie I saw that night, but I'll always remember the Pathe newsreel.

Just to show you how far people would go in trying to take advantage of a situation, a friend gave me a copy of the *Thermopolis*

Independent Record. The headline read "The Tepee Theatre Scoops the World." Fred Curtis, the owner and publicist, had a chance to show off his flair and success. He wrote:

> The Tepee Theatre got a scoop on all the other shows of the state to show reels Sunday, Monday, and Tuesday of the bank holdup at Powell in which Earl Durand's career was ended. The Tepee brings this picture to its patrons only a week after the happenings transpired.

Then Fred gives himself a big publicist's pat on the back. "When it comes to up-to-date pictures, Fred Curtis beats them all."

If that isn't disgusting, I don't know what is.

Johnny Gawthrop was as close to a saint as any young man I have ever known. He was just perfect—a good athlete, a good scholar, an excellent employee. He was good at tennis, clever at golf, and a terrific skier. We all held him in the highest regard, expecting a brilliant future for the young fellow. Everybody just loved him. It was a joy to be in his company. Soon after, I met his fiancée, Dixie Derby. She went to pieces. I had to console her and I wasn't in such good shape myself. It took all the effort I could muster to keep from breaking down in tears. She thought I was Johnny's best friend.

Earl's father was a customer of ours. I had to wait on him the first time he came into the bank after the events. I didn't know what to do or say, so I didn't say anything. The poor fellow was grief-stricken. A few months later I heard the farm was sold and the family moved away—where, I don't know.

At first I didn't realize that this event had captured the public imagination. Curiosity-seekers plagued us all summer. Even though Powell was about twenty-five miles out of the way, many headed for Cody and Yellowstone detoured and stopped off, another spot to photograph and tell the folks about back home. When I arrived each morning, there would be a bunch of people snapping pictures with their brand-new Kodak box cameras. I got a tremendous number of letters from people I didn't know, many of the envelopes stuffed with articles from their local newspapers about the events. The letters all wished me and the others involved well.

Earl Durand became a folk hero of sorts. A group in Billings, Montana, proposed erecting a monument in the Beartooth Mountains for him. Powell people notified them that a monument to Durand would be blown to bits the next day. So the plan was abandoned.

Twenty-one years later I became vice-president of St. Olaf College in Northfield, Minnesota. Jesse James and his gang had robbed a bank there years ago. The chamber of commerce held what they called "Jesse James Days" every year with a big parade, festival, and a reenactment of the robbery. Having gone through a similar event, I met with the chamber members and said, "Here you are trying to make a hero of this man. To me he was nothing but a villain who terrorized people and broke the law." I described what had happened to me in Powell. So they changed the name of the event to "The Defeat of Jesse James."

R.A. NELSON

BANK PRESIDENT

End of the Trail for Killer Durand—The First National Bank of Powell [was] surrounded by curious throngs a few minutes after the mountain desperado died with his boots on in a bloody gun battle that blocked his attempt at escape after robbing the bank.

Denver Post, March 25

I KNEW EARL FOR YEARS, but not well. I had heard a lot about him. Earl's father, Walter, was active in civic organizations, as I was. He was a bank customer for many years.

As a boy Earl had listened wide-eyed to the old-timers tell stories of the men who rode the trail with Wyoming's infamous outlaw band, the "Wild Bunch." When Earl's childhood friends grew into their teens and the games of "shootout" were replaced by interest in cars, jobs, and girls, Durand roved alone through the woods in the ways of the men of legend. The day he came back to town he single-handedly held up a bank in broad daylight, something not even Kid Curry had ever done.

My wife and I were at the Teton Theatre enjoying a movie the night Earl escaped from the Cody jail and killed the two lawmen. The movie stopped and the lights went on. Don Wright hurried to the front of the theater and told the crowd, "Earl Durand just killed Chuck Lewis and D.M. Baker. We're raising a posse. We need volunteers. Any man good with a rifle, report to City Hall and be sworn in." That was the first I heard about what Durand had done. There was nothing else talked about in Powell for several days. I never once thought of him coming back and robbing the bank. I assumed the law would probably catch him soon and put him back in jail.

The Billings Gazette had just set up the Wyoming Heroes Fund for the families of the four men Durand killed. I got a call from Governor Smith's office. The aide said the governor was asked to endorse the idea of a committee to distribute the funds and wanted to know what I thought of the idea. I said I thought it was fitting and would see to it that the civic organizations of Powell and the county would endorse it. That same morning, Friday it was, March 24, I mailed two twenty-five-dollar checks to the Fund—one from the Powell Boosters Club and one from the bank—and wrote a note to the editor: "I think the *Gazette* is doing a fine thing in sponsoring this fund. The families of these men certainly will need whatever help can be given them, and no one deserves it more. The people in this country, I am sure, will welcome an opportunity to help on this, and we are proud of the *Gazette* for leading the way."

My desk was in a little open place right beside the entrance and to the side of the lobby. I faced the front door. I was talking to one of the customers, the fellow who owned the lumberyard, Harry Hecht, and I saw Earl come in with a rifle in his hand and a revolver stuck in his belt. He knew me and I knew him. "Hello, Nelson," is all he said at first. He looked wild, demented is the word. It was obvious to me what he wanted. "Stick up your hands, everybody. I won't kill you if you do what I say, but no monkey business. Get over here," he said, motioning to the wall, "and line up with your faces to the wall."

The noise of his .30–.30 rifle going off inside the cavern of a bank was deafening. After he fired a few shots my ears felt like they were stuffed with cotton. I couldn't differentiate sounds. When Earl started shouting at us, I couldn't make out what he was saying. He motioned to us and that is how I made out what he wanted us to do.

After he terrorized us for a time, shot out all the windows and light fixtures, and took the money he wanted, he tied the three of us together, Gawthrop, Knutson, and me. "Come on, boys, we're going out," he said, tugging on the rope. Earl gathered up the money bags from the desk as we passed. Pushing Gawthrop out ahead, Durand came out with me and Knutson, his rifle in his right hand and the money bags clutched in his left. Just before we opened the door and stepped out, Earl warned us, "You try to get away, I'll plug you." He jerked the rope, throwing us all a little off balance, to let us know he was in charge, as if we didn't know.

As soon as young Johnny Gawthrop stepped down to the sidewalk bullets started flying, striking the windows and walls behind us. Chips of brick and concrete splinters showered the pavement, and we had another worry, another source of danger and harm. Durand's shooting in the bank had attracted the attention of all the folk within earshot. When we walked out people were hiding around every corner, waiting for him. Earl started shooting around Johnny, using the poor boy as a shield, and sure enough the shield took the bullet intended for Durand. Earl was firing up and down the street. He held the trigger down and every time he pumped the lever a shot rang out. But he was firing wildly. There was nobody in sight to shoot at. All Knutson and I could do was stay there tied to each other and to Johnny, who was still alive and writhing in excruciating pain, his heart's blood pulsing out of a wound that was invisible to us, somewhere under his suit jacket and white shirt. It tore my heart out to see the poor boy suffering so, his young, promising life spilling out into a thick pool on the sidewalk. I was never so sad for another person before in my life. I had known John since he was born. I wasn't more than two years older than him. Our parents had been friends for thirty years. They knew each other back in Iowa before they came to Wyoming. He was like my younger brother. I saw his eyes glaze over and a few seconds later they fluttered shut. He was still breathing, but I could tell that he didn't have long to live. And right next to the dying Johnny Gawthrop stood Durand, firing away, intent on making good his getaway.

Then Durand fell to the pavement and ended up in a sitting position. He let out a loud grunt. I was right beside him when he was shot. He crawled back into the bank on his hands and knees, tugged at the revolver, and shot himself. After Durand dropped the rope, I was able to work a hand loose. I don't remember exactly what I did after he went into the bank. When I heard his gun go off, I thought he was shooting the people inside. Later Maury Knutson

After the hold-up, bank officials R.A. Nelson, Maurice Knutson, and Edgar Swallow demonstrate for newspaper photographers how Durand tied their hands. Swallow stands in for John Gawthrop, the bank clerk who was killed. (Park County Historical Archives)

told me that I said, "I want to make sure he is dead." The first thing I know, I was standing over Durand with his rifle in my hands and there were two bullet holes in his head. I don't dispute the fact that I shot him; I just have no recollection of it.

Then the reporters besieged us. The first to arrive was a guy from the *Billings Gazette* who worked in town. He was followed by the staff of the *Powell Tribune*, folks I knew very well. Soon the whole brood of reporters and photographers who had been up on the Beartooth arrived, notepads, pencils, and cameras itching to go. I don't know how many times I repeated what had happened. I was in a fog the whole time. I felt like my life had changed, but I didn't know how. We posed in the bank for a photographer. The next day the *Denver Post* ran a picture of me, Maury Knutson, and Edgar Swallow over the caption:

> Three officials of the First National Bank of Powell escaped with their lives because they did exactly what Durand told them to do. They are shown here demonstrating how Durand tied their wrists together and attempted to use them as a shield as he left the bank. Bob Nelson (left), president, Maurice Knutson, cashier, and Edgar Swallow (right) are re-enacting the exciting drama. Swallow took the place occupied by John Gawthrop, 20, bank clerk, who was slain in the gun battle that ended Durand's bloody crime career.

THERE WAS ALSO A STORY that they printed signed with my name. Believe me, I didn't write it. I just told the reporter what happened and he went and said I wrote it.

After the reporters left I felt completely drained. Never in my life did I ever dream of taking a gun to a man, and I had. It's the sort of thing that gives you headaches when you think about it.

When the whole thing was totaled up, the Durand campaign cost the state of Wyoming at least $39,000. There were peace officer indemnities, and the state legislature passed a special relief appropriation to aid the families of the slain officers. And there were actual expenses of the chase—food, ammunition, rental of horses, salaries for all the men, gas for cars and Bill Monday's plane. But in the end the money was the least of it. The real costs were in human lives and suffering. All of us involved were scarred in some way. We all recovered, of course. But we'll never forget, and never be quite the same. I hear that soldiers go through much the same thing, but at least for them there is a purpose. Our encounter with Earl Durand was senseless, killing for no good reason at all.

TIP COX

THE BOY WHO KILLED EARL DURAND

SPATTERING BULLETS FELL THE NATION'S WORST OUTLAW
Denver Post headline, March 25

A trip to Denver by air Saturday morning to make his appearance before the KLZ microphone of the Columbia national hookup, thence to New York City to appear in the Tuesday night's "We the People" were the immediate rewards that came to this Powell high school junior as a result of his participation in the "stop Durand" effort among Powell's citizens at 1:45 P.M. last Friday.

But that will not be all the recognition that goes to this boy. In motion picture news reels now showing from coast to coast the Cox boy will have a most conspicuous part. He re-enacted the shooting scene at the Gillette filling station last Friday as best he could for news and press service photographers, and this 17-year-old Powell lad, who never before had had more than the average boy's experience at handling a gun, was suddenly whiffed into the national limelight as a marksman.

Powell Tribune, March 30

EARL WAS THE FRIEND OF a good friend of mine, a kid by the name of Tom Spint. He lived near the Durands. I spent the weekend at Tom's a couple of times. Once when I was there, Durand came over and we hiked up into the hills above the canal north of the Spint place with our rifles. People dumped trash there, and we used anything we could find for targets to shoot at. When we found a set of six or eight cracked dinner plates, we tossed them plates up in the air as high as we could and Earl shot them, then hit most of the shards before they reached the ground.

I had heard about his shooting, but that was the first time I'd ever seen him. I had my doubts about some of the stories, but after I saw him demolish three of those plates, I believed them. I've never seen anybody shoot like that outside of Remington Arms exhibition shots. Earl left the rest of the plates to us, threw them up for us himself. He wasn't selfish at all about them. All the kids in Powell thought Earl was a swell guy.

My folks had just moved to a ranch in the Lakeview country above Cody. I went to school in Powell so I could play on the football team. During the week I stayed with an aunt and uncle; I went home weekends. I'd catch the bus on Friday afternoons, either at three or five o'clock, and Dad would meet me at the Cody stop.

It was a nice early-spring Friday in late March. I was in the cafeteria at school eating lunch with Tom Spint. I said, "All I have the rest of the day is study hall and a shop class." Tom said, "If I was you, I'd catch the early bus home."

"I've got two and a half hours to kill. I'll go to town. That's better than staying around here."

So I wandered around the streets of Powell, looking in shop windows, just kind of loitering about, bumming you might call it. If ever a boy was going to be taught a lesson about playing hooky, I was about to. I was just going past the Texaco filling station. There were four or five people standing around, agitated, looking at the bank. You know how you'll come on a crowd and everybody is looking at something? You'll stop and take a look, too. Well, I did like the others. They had seen someone run in the bank all wild-looking and strange-acting. Suddenly we heard some shots. Otis Gillette, the man who owned the station, shouted, "Get inside and lay down on the floor! The bank is being held up." And I did. But like a dumb kid, I'm kneeling in the doorway peering out.

There was old Mr. Spot, that was his name, standing in front of the filling station. Everyone got inside the station and laid on the floor except him and me. Mr. Spot wasn't going to lay on the floor for anybody. He came in and sat on a stool, watching from a window. Two bullets crashed through the glass and some of the slivers cut his cheek. Mr. Spot, he sat there with a funny expression on his face, like his dinner was repeating on him. Then blood started to trickle down his face and he touched it with his fingertips. "My God!" he said. "I'm shot!" and he fainted, fell off the stool. I didn't know the other men who were in the garage. A bullet lodged in Gillette's receipt ledger; the other hit a girlie calendar, got her right in the kisser.

Mr. Gillette turned his radio on to the Billings station, kind of a reflex, to see if he could find out what was going on. At first it seemed like the radio wasn't working, then it sounded like you could hear firecrackers going off. We realized that, the dangedest thing, the robbery was being broadcast just as it was happening! Why, we were startled beyond belief. How in the world could the radio station know that there was a robbery going on, and how could they broadcast it? We thought that some bizarre miracle was happening, and that didn't make us any the more comfortable. It reminded me of some radio program acted out to scare the bejesus out of you, like "The Shadow" or worse yet, that horror they had on last Halloween, "The War of the Worlds," which had us terrified that the earth had been invaded by Martians. It turned out that a reporter who lived in Powell was in a drugstore around the corner from the bank. He hooked up with a radio station by phone and told what was happening.

I was nearest the door so I was the only one with a view down the street. I peeked out and saw the oddest thing. An eighty-year-old woman was tottering toward the bank waving a big Colt .45—it was swaying from side to side like a corn leaf in the wind. I just watched in amazement. No one else in the station could see her, but I told them what I saw. We found out later she was Mr. Nelson's aunt, who lived a block or two away. When she heard the bank was being robbed, she opened an old trunk, dragged out a navy Colt revolver, and joined the fray.

Those days folks around Powell were pretty jittery. Like many other businessmen, Mr. Gillette had brought a rifle to the station. Without my realizing it, he had taken his rifle down off the shelf.

Then he passed it—a .348 Winchester lever action with hammer—up to me with a handful of shells. I loaded the rifle, waiting for the robber to come out of the bank.

After Johnny Gawthrop stepped out of the bank and was shot, a wild-looking man followed right behind him and fired his rifle up the street in the direction the shot came from. I recognized him as Durand. We were utterly surprised that it was him because we all believed he was up in the Beartooths. There it was again, that strange sense of a world the imagination might make, replacing the world of everyday reality. Just like when the radio was broadcasting the robbery. How could these things be?

It looked pretty much like I would be the one to kill the killer. I had a premonition of it the second I saw it was Earl Durand. I'm kneeling and trying to draw a bead on Durand. I used the doorjamb as a brace and swivel. I felt nervous, like I did when I shot my first deer. I also felt like I wasn't really where I was, couldn't possibly be doing what I was doing. It was hard to take calm and steady aim. Us kids were used to guns and hunting. So at the same time I didn't even think that I was doing anything unusual. Earl spied me and he's coming down with his rifle. Its barrel was still smoking and looked as big around as a stovepipe. That was the first time I ever looked down the barrel of a loaded gun. Then I squeezed the trigger. The rifle cracked. Earl clutched at his chest and spun to the ground. His gun went off again, but the shot didn't do any harm. He ended up sitting with his legs stretched out in front of him. I lowered the rifle, then raised it, aimed, and squeezed again. I had been in such a hurry that I forgot to work the lever and put a shell in the chamber. By the time I got another shell in, Earl had crawled back into the bank. Later, the coroner said the bullet caught him on the right side high on the chest, and you could stick both fists in the hole where it came out his back.

How he had the strength or willpower to drag himself back into the bank, take his revolver out of its holster, put it to his neck, and fire, I'll never know. What I did I was sorry I had to do, but it had to be done. Durand was drawing a bead on me. Afterwards I felt sort of sick. It was the first time I ever shot at anybody. Durand's rampage was over. He was dead and five men were dead.

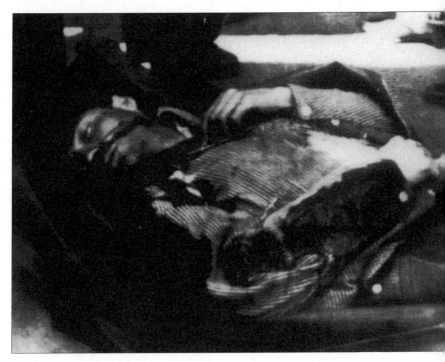

Earl Durand's body was taken out of the bank and laid on the sidewalk outside.
(Park County Historical Archives)

After the shooting stopped I ran across the street. Durand was lying inside the bank doorway. People came running out from everywhere, swarming into the bank. Suddenly the place was in an uproar. I heard somebody yell, "Get a car! Gawthrop is still alive!" I knew Johnny Gawthrop well. He went on our football trips as a trainer. He wrapped our ankles and knees. Everyone knew him and liked him. I turned around and there was a brand-new Buick with its wing windows broken out. The keys were in it. So I got in and started it up. Some people laid Gawthrop in the back seat. Someone, I don't know who it was, crawled in and held Johnny as I drove to the hospital. Someone must have called ahead to let them know we were coming because when we drove up a doctor and nurse were waiting at the entrance. But Gawthrop was dying, breathing his last few breaths, gasps with the sound of gargling. I can see it all like it happened five seconds ago.

MY FOLKS DIDN'T KNOW what happened at the bank until they heard it on the radio later that afternoon. I was surrounded by reporters and people asking questions. I didn't even think to call and tell my folks what I had done. After they heard the news they got in the car and drove to Powell looking for me. The only question my father asked about it was, "What in the hell did you do it for?" And I told him. I went home with them to Cody. That might have been the end of it, but later that evening we got a call at home from a reporter from the *Denver Post*. I gave him my version of what happened.

Then he asked to speak to my father. I was surprised, but I gave Dad the phone. The reporter invited me to be on the radio program "The People Speak." The famous news commentator and announcer Gabriel Heater was the host. It had been on radio about ten years by then. There were celebrities on every week and skits that reenacted events in the news—like newsreels without pictures. That's what they wanted me to come and do. They wanted me to act out what had happened in front of the bank. They were going to present me as the boy who shot Earl Durand.

At first my dad wasn't going to let me go, but finally he thought a trip to New York might be a good experience for me. The radio show paid all my expenses and gave me a little spending money. The sports announcer from KLZ in Denver went with me. He was in charge of me the whole time. I flew from Cody to Denver. It was the first time I ever flew on a plane. Then we took the train to New York. It was swell. I had heard about how wonderful travel by train was and it was even better than I thought. I saw all the country between Denver and New York coming and going. It wasn't anything like I was used to, no mountains and hardly a hill in sight. But it was America and it was something to see. When we got to New York City there was a lot of reporters, newsreel crews, and all. They kept us busy for quite a while with questions.

I was excited about being on radio, but of course I wasn't the main attraction, not by a long shot. First on came Mr. Bill "Bojangles" Robinson talking up a new play he was starring in on Broadway, *Hot Mikado*. Mr. Robinson explained that the play come from another play by two Englishmen named Gilbert and Sullivan, but it

Tip Cox, the teenager who shot Durand, poses in front of the First National Bank of Powell. Note the bullet hole in the door. (Park County Historical Archives)

had modern songs and music. The truth is, I couldn't make a whole lot of sense out of what he described. Then some starlets and actors came on and sang a song from the play. That didn't enlighten me any either, but the audience in the radio studio ate it up. Then Bojangles up and did a tap dance. Imagine that, tap dancing on the radio. But he was sure graceful and fast. He made it look easy as pie. I believe he was one of the best tap dancers ever. Meeting Bill Robinson was okay.

Then on came Barney Oldfield, the famous race car driver. He impressed me most. Every boy in the country knew about him—he was as well known in racing as Babe Ruth was in baseball or Bronco

Nagursky in football. Whenever a cop stopped a speedster, he would ask, "Say, who do ya think you are, Barney Oldfield?" By now Barney wasn't racing any more. He worked for Firestone tires, plugging safety on the road. That's what he was on the show to do. But there was a lot of jabbering between him and Mr. Heater and that's really what the people wanted to hear. Oldfield had his famous cheroot clamped in his jaw and his lucky red-and-white-checked Texas bandanna around his neck. Gabriel Heater said a little poem about the cigar.

> *"Yes, Barney's here!" they cried,*
> *"The starting bomb can shoot!*
> *'Twouldn't be no race at all without*
> *Oldfield and his cheroot!"*

Barney told about the most exciting race he had ever run. It was the 1914 Cactus Derby, "the roughest road race in the U.S. of A.," he said. The race started in Los Angeles and ended, after three days and 671 miles of sagebrush and potholes, in Phoenix, Arizona. There were no roads whatsoever through most of the route. The racers ran through wind, blinding alkali dust, desert sand, mud, rocks, snow, boulders in gullies—the terrain Barney described reminded me a lot of the rugged backcountry up where I lived.

Barney said the excitement of the second day was crossing a railway trestle across the Colorado River on heavy two-by-fourteen planks. On and on, disaster after disaster. As a climax the cars had to cross two rivers, straight through the water. A mule skinner and his team that happened by towed Barney's stalled car out of the swollen waters and thick mud of the New River just fifteen miles shy of the finish line: a miracle and just in the nick of time.

Barney told the story with such life that he had the whole audience waiting for the climax. When he told about passing the two cars that had passed him in the river, the audience let out a cheer, just like the race was happening now, not twenty-four years ago. And I was as thrilled as anyone. Then he talked about safe driving.

My part in the program came last. It was a skit called "The End of Earl Durand." Gabriel Heater told the events, and when it came to where Earl was escaping from the bank, I spoke up and said what I had done. I was awful nervous. Fortunately, my speech was typed out and I rehearsed it with a lady three or four times before the program. "Don't be nervous," she kept telling me. "Relax." But it was over and done with in a few minutes. The skit was like a newsreel, with sound effects and the speakers taking the place of movies. All the time there were guys working dials, giving hand signals, and one was in charge of the sound effects.

After he heard my skit Barney Oldfield shook my hand and told me he was happy to meet a brave young man. They talk about the magic of radio. I don't know about magic, but it was sure exciting.

I went to Jack and Charlie's 21 Club half a dozen times with the announcer from Denver. I would have rather come with one of them starlets in the Club and drank whiskey instead of ginger ale. I had never seen any actors or celebrities or famous beauties in Powell, but here they were. Almost every person who walked in the door, he told me who they were. He also told me something about the ones I wasn't familiar with. I enjoyed that best of all. Of course he took me to the Empire State Building and the Statue of Liberty, the Museum of Natural History, and some sporting events at Madison Square Garden, but what impressed me most was the 21 Club. I never saw anything like that before or since. I was in New York City a week. New York was quite a place for a country kid.

WHEN I GOT BACK TO SCHOOL, there was not a word about my killing Durand or my trip to New York, which was just fine, though I could tell that a lot of kids were just busting to bring it up. The only reaction I got from anybody was from my geology teacher. For some reason my shooting Durand really upset him. He took me down in the school basement where we had a few words over it. I told him, "You're the first guy that's ever mentioned this since I came home." Then I told him to drop the subject and that was the end of it.

I'm sorry I *had* to kill Earl Durand, but I'm not sorry I did it. He wasn't the same Earl Durand I had gone plinkin' with. And it seems funny, but that was the last time I ever played hooky from school. I actually took school more seriously afterwards. I had seen New York City, and I knew that I'd better apply myself more to my endeavors if I expected to get anywhere in life.

THE END

But Earl Durand is gone. He forfeited his right
to live, and his life is a closed chapter. Powell people,
in a united way, went to heal these wounds, and in that
spirit, so far as we are concerned the narrative of the
fugitive Earl Durand's exploits has been told.

Powell Tribune, March 30, 1939

Ray Easton

Undertaker and County Coroner

> Thousands View Body of Killer in Coroner's Home at
> Powell (Crime Never Pays).... Wyoming's "Tarzan
> of the Tetons" made a bloody entrance on the stage
> of crime. His exit was equally gory and sensational.
> *Denver Post*, March 25

AFTER I GOT MY LICENSE as a mortician, I started in Denver then came
up to Sheridan, Wyoming, in 1924 to work for Mr. Champion in
his funeral business. I worked for him until 1930 when he and I
bought the Powell Funeral Home and operated it as partners until
1936. I bought him out, changed the name to Easton's Funeral
Home. At the time of the Durand episode I was running it alone.
The town was small, population of only twelve hundred souls. There
wasn't enough business at the funeral home, so I worked part-time in
a hardware store. I knew Earl since he was about seventeen. He used
to come into the store and talk guns. He was a gun fan. It was a
hobby with him, a passion.

Powell is a government town, an irrigation district. The Bureau
of Reclamation laid it out. They set aside some government-owned
lots for the Heart Mountain Rod and Gun Club. The building was
an indoor .22-rifle range, a drop-sided affair one hundred fifty feet
long. We had government guns and were furnished government
ammunition as part of a surplus program. Earl was a member, though
he didn't shoot every week. I also knew him through the gun club.

There were only a few deaths a month around here. I handled
the business and hired assistants to work by the job. But suddenly

within a week I had six bodies to prepare for burial, an autopsy, and an inquest to conduct. Six men were killed by the rifle, not a natural death in the bunch. That set a record for modern times in Wyoming. Not only did we have few deaths in this neck of the woods, we had no deliberate killings. There would be the rare accidental hunting death. This wasn't the West of the Western magazines kids and men all over the country love and eat up. This was farmers working hard, living sober, churchly, plain lives, and making a living from their crops. So I damn sure was not ready to lay out six bodies all dead from bullet wounds, not ready for the impression those eleven days would make on me.

It's downright sobering to see the destructive power of a bullet. When my father was teaching me about guns, he told me, "A well-thrown stone can take out an eye or crack a skull. And what do your arrows do when you shoot at your mother's old Sears catalogue? Son, it's the speed of the object that does the killing. A bullet moves so fast, the human eye can't see it. Guns are made to speed little, deadly rifle slugs to their targets. Be careful with guns, son. Be mighty careful." We do enough hunting up here to know what happens when a rifle slug hits an animal. A man's body is no different. The same things happen. Death by rifle is the worst. There's so much damage. I never expected to see so many beloved friends and innocent people suddenly destroyed by the gun.

WE REACHED BAKER ABOUT two hours after he died. It was cold that night and snowing one of them wet snows, the kind that melts the quickest and feels the coldest. Poor Baker was stiff as a board. He had hardly any blood left in him. It must have gushed out all at once. He'd been struck in the head and died instantly.

My assistant and I transported him to the funeral home and started work on him right away. I had to prepare the body for burial. There was no public viewing. Baker's family chose to remember him as he had looked when he was alive rather than by what they would see now.

We knew Chuck Lewis was at the hospital, dying. At eleven-thirty that night the call came. "Come pick up Lewis." The bullet pierced his side just below the heart and shattered on the backbone, cutting the spinal cord. Lewis was well-known and well liked. Several hundred people from all over northern Wyoming and southern Montana crowded into the American Legion Hall for the service held that Sunday morning and, if you can believe it, a couple thousand were at the funeral. There were two hundred wreaths and sprays crowded around the casket. It was a full military funeral. The cortege was so long that cars were still arriving at the cemetery after the casket had been lowered into the ground.

General Maurice, Lewis's commanding officer in World War I, eulogized Lewis in a letter to the *Casper Tribune*:

> I am moved to write to you about Marshal Chuck Lewis of Powell, killed by a desperado. I am greatly grieved and shocked. Chuck Lewis was first sergeant of battery F in the old 148th field artillery—the Wyoming regiment of the World War, which I had the honor to command in France. Chuck Lewis, as we knew him, was a top-notch soldier; faithful, efficient and lovable. They didn't make them any better. I knew him long and well and had a deep affection for him, and I just want to pay tribute to the memory of a splendid soldier and a gentleman. It is typical that he died in the line of duty, because he was the sort that always did his duty, when a soldier in his country's service, or when an officer in his town's service.
>
> "I want you to know of this feeling of the high esteem and affection felt by his old commanding officer towards a gallant soldier."

And that was pretty much the opinions around here about Chuck Lewis. He might have been a little foolhardy and reckless, and he was certainly mistaken in his appraisal of Earl Durand, but he was as solid as a hickory nut, as slick as an eel. You could always count on Chuck to do what was expected of him.

IT WAS SEVERAL DAYS BEFORE Sheriff Blackburn arrived on the scene. But when he did, I'll tell you now, it was pretty Sam serious. The sheriff deputized men for the posse and you had no choice. You were a citizen and if the sheriff said so, you went. You're going and you don't know whether you're coming back or not.

I was the county coroner so I had to stay in town. There were already two law officers dead and buried. I wasn't allowed on the posse. You could almost say the dead were piling up faster than we could bury them. No sooner did we finish up the funerals of two fine folk and old friends than two possemen stepped into Earl's line of fire. I didn't know either of the two men. Argento and Linabary's bodies lay where they fell all afternoon, through the night till next morning. The buzzards were getting ready for breakfast, ravens I believe it was. Frank Blackburn contacted me and asked me to bring my rig and cart them in. When my helper got there he took out two rubber-lined canvas body bags, laid one alongside each body. "Gimme a hand, will ya? Put these bodies in the bags." Four possemen helped him load them in the car. When he got back I had two bodies to examine and store. Since both of them were being shipped elsewhere, I just put them on ice.

Durand had hit both men right in the heart. It was nothing but ghastly. He was a marksman and as far as Durand being a hunter, Argento and Linabary were big as all the bears he killed. With those two quote-unquote possemen walking right into his gun barrel, they were like still targets at close range. And a man will die from one bullet where a bear takes a few. He killed those men without any excuse I can see.

All I know about Argento is he was from Italy. I was told he was an expert at handling dynamite and explosives, worked on blasting projects all over the state. The oldest son, Emil, was a grown man. He took his father's body back to Meeteetse where the family lived. Argento had children all the way down to six.

And Orville Linabary. He worked in the oil field and cowboyed. Linabary was a well-known rodeo rider. So that tells you about him. Linabary was buried at Riverside Cemetery in Cody three days after he was shot. There was a large crowd. The reverend preached a word of eulogy over the flower-covered casket. But you couldn't top what Linabary's mother said later to a reporter, while people were offering her their condolences. We were crowded about. She spoke in an unusually loud voice, the kind some women develop from calling men in from the fields. So we couldn't help overhearing. "I was not surprised that my son was killed in a battle with Durand in the mountains," she told the reporter. "Orville was just that way. Always courting danger." You would expect Mrs. Linabary to have been greatly shocked when she heard on the radio that her son had been shot. But she said, "I always knew that his life would end in some such tragic manner. He was just that way." Peoples' jaws just dropped. It threw such a strange light on the events. But then none of us was really much surprised about Earl's end either. We could see it way back in his beginnings if we had been willing to look.

IT WENT ON FOR SO LONG. We had days of it. Toward the end the United Press and the Associated Press called me every hour, it seemed. I didn't get much sleep and I couldn't tell them anything they didn't already know. I carried a rifle in my car all during Earl's spree. My wife's rifle was loaned out to someone up on the posse, or she would have had hers loaded and propped by the door at home. Both of us hunted. We always kept unloaded guns in the house.

There was a rough element in Billings, Montana, and folks in town had remarked that it would be no surprise if the gang tried to hold up the bank because all the law was out of town. We weren't particularly worried about Earl coming back into Powell; we thought he was still in the mountains. Even so, nearly everybody was ready to get him.

My two-door Ford was out in front of the funeral home on the eleventh day. I kept a little metal stretcher and my rifle in it. I was reading a magazine in the parlor, with the double doors at the entryway open. It was nice and warm just like a summer day, even though it was March. Then I heard all this shooting going on. From where I was, the bank was half a block east and one block south, so it was out of my sight. I stepped out and asked the fellas working at the lumberyard next door—one of them used to go on calls with me— I asked, "What's going on?"

"Well, I guess somebody's holding up the bank."

I came inside and called my wife, Irma, at home to tell her what was happening. I said, "There's shooting downtown. Sounds like it's coming from the bank. I'd better go over and see what's going on," and I walked to the bank.

She said to me, "You just be careful, Ray."

She told me that right after she hung up, the phone rang again, this time from Dr. Stahn, the dentist, who had been held in the bank when Earl went berserk. He was trying to get in touch with me to let me know there was a man dead, but he only knew my home phone number. He didn't know I was already on my way over. He didn't identify himself, but Irma recognized his voice. He was excited. He had a cigarette in his mouth and couldn't blow out the smoke. He was choking on the smoke. He sputtered, "Irma, he's dead down here at the bank!" Of course, she thought Dr. Stahn meant I was dead. She dashed out and pulled over the first car to come along. It was Ray Baird, the editor of the *Powell Tribune*. She said, "Ray, take me to the funeral home!" She rode on the running board, didn't even get in. Ray wasn't known to be a very good driver anyway. He almost turned the car over going around the corner. Ray couldn't get the car to stop. His feet probably rummaged around from pedal to pedal, and he nearly threw my wife off. Irma jumped off while the car was still moving.

After the shooting stopped, I went into the Wyoming Hotel, called my assistant, and had him drive my car over. When we heard that Johnny Gawthrop was dead, I sent him to pick up the boy at the hospital and take him to the funeral home. Just as Irma reached the funeral home, my car pulled up. The driver was bringing Johnny Gawthrop in. My wife still thought the corpse was me, sort of a mortician's wife's nightmare-come-true. "Ray," she cried, recoiling in stunned grief.

The driver said, "This is poor Johnny Gawthrop, Mrs. Easton. He's dead. Ray is at the bank. Earl Durand is dead."

She was so confused by what he said and the way he said it, she still thought I was dead.

I had stayed behind at the bank with Earl's body.

When I finally got back to the parlor, I put my gun away. Things had quieted down for the moment. There was no more shooting. I had two more bodies to prepare, two viewings to set up. Earl had bullet wounds in the cheek and neck I had to make presentable. The chest wound I just closed up enough to make do. I drained the blood from both bodies. Being a big man, Durand had a lot of blood, but since he had been shot three times, he had already lost a lot of blood out on the sidewalk and then inside the vestibule of the bank. But that was made up for in the time I had to spend closing the wounds, embalming the cadaver, and writing the coroner's report, which called for a lot more details than the ordinary death certificate.

While I was in the middle of all this work, in barges Bob White, a guy I knew a little from down Greybull way. He was an outfitter and a guide down in that part of the Big Horns and had a particular reputation as a taxidermist for the trophies of Hollywood and the rich. He did a hell of a business in trophy heads—bighorn sheep, elk, moose, deer—and anything a hunter wanted stuffed. He was also a licensed mortician. White was part of the posse. My helper told me he had run into White in the Beartooths when he picked up those two men who put themselves in Durand's sights. Now Durand had joined them in the happy hunting ground.

White was carrying a cardboard box. He had a jar of Vaseline and a bag of plaster of Paris. He said, "Hello, Ray. Business is boomin', I hear."

"What do you want, Bob?" I asked, inquisitive as all get-out. "Come to stuff Durand for the state rotunda? Since you was picked to mount that buffalo for the state capitol, you got the idea that you have a right to everything that's dead."

"No, I don't want to stuff him. Ray, it'll just take me fifteen minutes. I'll make a mold. My interests are in the history. I'll give you a mask when I'm done."

"What in tarnation!" I said. "If you ain't the gol-dangest old coot! You come down here to make a death mask of Earl Durand's face!" The gall of the guy. "I'm here killing myself trying to get the body ready for viewing, and you want to play with the cadaver!"

He says, with a twinkle in his eye, "I got an idea. What with the World's Fair in San Francisco in full swing and this story hot in the papers, I think I can get folks to come by to gawk for a dime a time. What do you think?"

"I think you're quite a stinker, that's what I think. But give me a hand stitching Durand up and getting him presentable. Make damn certain you wipe off all the Vaseline. And I mean all of it, you rascal. If this ever gets out, I'll hunt you down like the rat you are!" I said, "Go ahead. I don't want no damned death mask of a murderer." As we worked, I asked, "Why don't you sell them as souvenirs?"

"I hadn't thought of that! They'll sell like hotcakes. I'll ship a few hundred of them to the World's Fair. You got a hell of an idea, Ray. Wanna go partners?"

"Get out of here, you faker."

It was like an undertakers' hoot. We roared with laughter. The gumption of the guy. I knew his idea would never get anywhere so I wasn't too worried. And I sure needed his help. There was a line of people growing outside who wanted to be able to say they had seen that badman Earl Durand laid out and getting his just deserts.

I dressed Durand in a brown burial suit. It fit him like it was tailor-made. Earl had bullet holes in the neck, cheek, and chest. I had to cover the hole in his cheek. The others were out of sight.

Everyone was drained and tired. The nervous excitement had been a lot more than what we were accustomed to in our quiet little spot on earth. It wasn't long, though, before crowds started congregating in town, sightseeing at all the points of interest in the afternoon's events, and everybody was an expert. Newspaper reporters came in from the mountains as quick as they could. They tore around town. Some were taking pictures. Others lined up and bickered around the pay phone in the Wyoming Hotel. They were calling their stories in to their newspapers. The reporters rushed to interview anyone they could find who had anything to do with the events—hotel guests, storekeepers—anyone they could get their hands on. They were bidding for snapshots of Durand dead. I had never seen anything like it in my life. Meanwhile, folks from Greybull, Meeteetse, Basin, Thermopolis, Cody, Deaver, Ralston, even from Montana—Billings, Red Lodge, all around—were arriving in trucks and cars. Soon there wasn't a place to park in town. As things developed, the funeral home was the last stop on the tour, the climax, you might call it. I had White make up one of those signs with a black background that you push white plastic letters into.

DURAND VIEWING
4:00

He lowered the shades and bolted the doors. There must have been a couple hundred people waiting at three o'clock so I had a notion of what to expect by four.

I made up another sign for inside the doorway:

GENTLEMEN

REMOVE YOUR HATS

PHOTOGRAPHS NOT PERMITTED

When we opened the doors, the Pathe News boys were filming the crowd and took a shot of me looking out over the scene. The reporter was right near me reading his script into a wire recorder. The line of people waiting to get in snaked down the steps, along the sidewalk, and clear around the block to the entrance again. Ordinarily we laid the deceased out for viewing in one of our two side parlors. But realizing the number of people who would want to lay eyes on the dead "Tarzan of the Tetons" so they'd have something to talk about in their old age, we set up the stand and casket in the foyer and arranged for the line to pass through on two sides and leave through the back hallway. In the meantime, I called City Hall and asked for some deputies to be posted inside and outside the mortuary. Feelings were running high—about Durand and about how the whole affair had been handled. I had to make sure the crowd didn't get out of hand. The crowd's mood changed from moment to moment. Sometimes it was angry, sometimes there was weeping, sometimes the folks were eager and excited, like they were going into a carnival freak show, which is pretty much what we had going on inside. The only thing missing was the barker and the price of admission.

Four officers were sent over to keep things peaceable. Even so, a lot of men refused to remove their hats, a couple of them spat on Durand's face, a few came through the line three or four times, and I grabbed one guy just as he was about to mutilate Durand's face with a piece of broken glass. The officers did a good job. Without them, I'm afraid the crowd would have turned ugly and done things they would have regretted later on. As it was, some of the behavior was enough to make you disgusted. Granted, there were a lot of fine and innocent people who died because of Durand. But the dead deserve a certain amount of respect, too, no matter who they are.

After a few hours, I decided to take a stroll and see how my fair town was behaving outside. As you might expect, there was even less decorum in the bars and restaurants and sidewalks than there was in the funeral home.

Everyone and everything had become an attraction. The posse-men involved in the whole ordeal were the center of throngs who heard them tell what had happened again and again. It was so fes-tive, you'd never think that what drew all these people were two more killings on top of four others Durand had committed. Folks wanted to hear every word, didn't want to miss a syllable. Folks felt like Powell was the center of the world's attention. It was pitiful.

The sheriff posted a guy at the parlor door with a counter. He used it for quite a while, stopped when his hand got sore. He reached over nine hundred before he quit, but that was early in the evening. The last person passed through the back door just after midnight.

Two or three thousand people, I would say. Where they all came from in our sparsely populated part of the country, I'll never know.

In the early hours of Saturday morning, after I pulled the blinds and locked up the office, I sat down at my old desk for a minute and let the events just wash over me and start settling into place. The whole thing added up to a sad commentary on mankind. Every step taken seemed to be another foolish mistake. You could almost say that around here there was life before Durand and life after Durand. You had to be awful careful about expressing your opinion. You never knew when you'd be talking to a person who saw things differ-ent from the way you did. There were folks around who thought Durand got a raw deal; he should have just been left alone to hunt and live his life in the mountains. So folks kept silent on the matter, which seemed to work out best for all.

BY MORNING EVERYTHING HAD turned back to the way it had been, except for the rubbish the crowds left all over town, the mess around the bank, and I had some extra work to get ready for. That next morning Dr. Mills came by and performed an autopsy on Johnny Gawthrop. I observed. The bullet had hit him in the right shoulder, traveled down, and carved a crater in the chest. Many believed that Durand shot Gawthrop, but the slug wasn't from Durand's rifle. There was a memorial service at the Methodist church, and John was buried Monday in Riverside Cemetery at Cody.

On Tuesday afternoon I convened the coroner's jury. Blackburn, Steadman, and I conducted the inquest in the matter of John

Gawthrop's death. Knutson, Nelson, and a couple of other men testified. Dr. Mills summarized his autopsy findings and his report was entered as evidence. The jury's finding: "Death was due to an accidental gunshot wound by persons unknown."

No inquest was necessary in Durand's case.

THE DURAND FAMILY WAS under a lot of strain. In an incident like this, there are many details to attend to, a lot of unexpected expenses. I would have had to charge them twenty-five dollars for digging the grave, but some of the neighbors went earlier in the day and dug one. Not an easy job, but that was the way for a lot of people in this part of the country. Digging a six-foot-deep hole, with the sides and bottom properly trimmed and tapered, is a hell of job. And Earl's grave had to be an extra foot long because he was six-two to start with and nearly a foot wider than the ordinary man. But these farmers were used to digging. There was always the irrigation ditches to be trimmed and shaped, spud cellars to be dug, foundations for outbuildings. These guys were strong, but you try tossing shovel after shovel of clay up over six feet from a narrow hole with no room to get a good swing.

The funeral service began at four o'clock Sunday afternoon and lasted about half an hour. Fifty people attended, including the family circle and old friends from Powell. Over Earl's rose-covered casket, the Methodist minister preached words of comfort using a verse from the Forty-sixth Psalm—"The Lord of Hosts is with us; the God of Jacob is our refuge"—as his text. He talked about how God helps us in times of trial, loss, and sadness, but I had the feeling his words didn't do much good. The Durand family all sat lost in grief.

When the minister finished, Laura Sunderwaite, Earl's sister, went to the pulpit and read a poem in memory of her brother. Before she recited the three short verses of Tennyson's "Crossing the Bar," she announced that at one time her brother had requested that the poem be read over his body when he was gone. Laura's reading of it was quite lovely. People wept.

A procession of about twenty cars, headlights on, escorted Earl's body to its place of final rest. There was no graveside service. Reverend

Pallbearers load Earl Durand's casket into the hearse in front of Easton's Funeral Home. (Park County Historical Archives)

Benedict read a scripture verse, offered a word of prayer, and Earl's body was consigned to the earth.

Under the headline "Funeral Held at Powell Sunday of Earl Durand" the March 30 issue of the *Powell Tribune* reported, "David Earl Durand was born January 3, 1913 at Rockville, Missouri, the only son of Walter and Effie Durand. It was during that same year that the family moved to Powell, Wyoming, and this has ever since been their home. Earl Durand's death on March 24, 1939, was at the age of 26 years, two months and fifteen days.

"As a child Earl Durand did much reading and re-reading of folk stories of many lands, also nature books of birds and flowers. As he grew older, his favorite books pertained to camping and woodcraft, world history and the Bible. Family members said of him, that he read the Bible through five times."

The day after the funeral, Laura went into town and visited at the *Tribune* to make a special request of R. T. Baird, the owner and editor. She had written a eulogy, a tribute to her brother's memory, and asked him if he would publish it in the next issue. Because of the unusual circumstances, Mr. Baird agreed to her request and published a final tribute to this highly regarded family for all to read. It appeared under the unfortunate headline "Laura Durand Sunderwaite Comes to Brother's Defense."

> The most outstanding characteristic of my brother was his love for the truth. In no time during the many years which I spent with him do I recall that he ever told a falsehood. He was brave, honorable, proud, and his word was a sacred bond to himself. And often he said that the only wealth a man needs is his word.
>
> He was a rather lonely youth. He had for friends only those who were clean in thought and speech.
>
> Earl was very fond of history, novels and plays; his favorite stories being *The Sign of the Cross, Mutiny on the Bounty,* and *David Copperfield.* On all his camping trips with his friends and family he was most helpful in building fires, making and erecting tents and pointing out unusual birds and flowers.
>
> Through all Earl's years he became the friend and champion of the young, the sick and the aged, often giving his dollar to one in need, remarking that they needed it, he didn't. Criminals of any kind were foreign to him; he saw only good in all.
>
> As he grew older he spent most of his time in the mountains. They were a sacred shrine of his faith; firmly believing he could worship God on a mountain-top under the brilliant stars, more truly than he could in a crowded church.
>
> His last fateful trip was made in accordance to his creed of helping to feed the poor.
>
> Thus ended the short span of a man who dared to live according to his convictions, ideals, and faith in his God."

Another thing about the newspaper, the *Powell Tribune.* In our part of the country, it is customary for the newspaper to print a "Card of Thanks" for bereaved families. The newspaper helps the families pick the right words. These are curt, formal, and follow a few formulas. The March 30 paper printed cards of thanks from the Gawthrops just above the one from Orville Linabary's family. On another page was the card from the Durands, brief and quiet:

We wish to express our gratitude to our many friends who have been such help and comfort to us in our great sorrow.

Mr. and Mrs. W. W. Durand

Mrs. G. A Sunderwaite

Mrs. W. A. Harkins

Mrs. Glen A. Gardiner

It touched me to read these cards.

WITH A SISTER'S KIND REMARKS and the card of thanks, Earl Durand disappeared from the press. Durand was buried at Crown Hill Cemetery in Powell, along with Chuck Lewis and D. M. Baker. As we did after any funeral, we placed a cast-iron marker on it, with the name of the deceased—a place-holder until the stone was carved. As it turned out, we had a devil of a time keeping a marker on Earl's grave. When the marker disappeared overnight, we had another one made. It was up for a few days, then it disappeared. This happened half a dozen times. I guess local kids or souvenir hunters who thronged the town all that spring and summer must have lifted it— as despicable a thing to do as that. It would be a rare person now who could direct you to the right grave if you wanted to see where Earl's earthly remains were laid to rest.

ACKNOWLEDGMENTS

I THANK RONNIE KNOPP, Milward Simpson, Oliver Steadman, Art Glasgow, Dick Smith, Ed McNeely, Vern Spencer, Mel Stonehouse, Bill Garlow, Harry Moore, Vastalee Dutton, Maurice Knutson, Bob (R.A.) Nelson, Tip Cox, and Ray and Irma Easton for making it possible for me to write this book. They spoke with me at length about what they did, what they said, and what they knew. I did not interview Virginia Turner. Her narrative comes from newspaper reports and conversations with others who knew her.

I am indebted to Park County historians Alta Mae Markham of the Park County library, Nancy Ruskowsky and Ester Murray of Cody, and Robert Koelling from Powell for their helpful comments. Jeanie Cook, director of the Park County Historical Association, led me to important information and made Association materials and photographs available. The staff at First National Bank of Powell, especially Dave Reetz, provided valuable photographs and a blueprint of the bank's interior and took me through fine points about events that day in the bank. The bank's history, *First National Bank of Powell: The History of a Bank, a Community, and a Family* by Robert Koelling also provided clarifications. Thanks to Janet Taggert (nee Blackburn), daughter of Frank Blackburn and society reporter for the *Cody Enterprise* at the time of the events who gave me useful information. Also thanks to Ann Cargill who provided information on Durand's death mask.

Heartfelt thanks to Mindy Keskinen, editor, whose eagle eye, friendly criticism, and insight saved me from goofs and improved the telling of this history. Any errors remaining are my responsibility.

Sources & Methods

I RELIED HEAVILY ON the first-hand interviews with people connected to the Durand incident, which I conducted between 1978 and 1981 in Park County, Wyoming, and Billings, Montana. Those taped interviews are housed in the author's collection.

I also have drawn facts and observations from newspapers and magazines published in 1939. I incorporated some supplemental material from these sources into the voice of the narrators. Other newspaper and magazine material appears as epigraphs. Some is quoted directly. These newspapers and magazines included:

Denver Post, March 22–March 27

Cody Enterprise, March 29

Powell Tribune, March 16, 23, and 30

Thermopolis Independent Record, March 30

Time, March 27

Official Detective, July 1939

AN EXAMPLE OF HOW I incorporated the supplemental newspaper material into the narrator's voice can be found in the Ray Easton chapter on pages 198–211.

The *Thermopolis Independent Record* of March 30, 1939, carried an article with this information:

> Newspaper writers and cameramen were tearing around, shooting pictures, putting in long distance calls, interviewing

excited people, bidding for snapshots taken of Durand right after the raid when he lay dead, ordering airplanes....

I blended that information with the Ray Easton interview to flesh out Easton's account, to provide the reader with addtional insight, and to create a smooth narrative. The narrator, Ray Easton, says in this book's text:

Newspaper reporters came in from the mountain as quick as they could. They tore around town. Some were taking pictures. Others lined up and bickered around the pay phone in the Wyoming Hotel. They were calling their stories in to their newspapers. The reporters rushed to interview anyone they could find who had anything to do with the events—hotel guests, storekeepers—anyone they could get their hands on. They were bidding for snapshots of Durand dead. I had never seen anything like it in my life.

INDEX

ABOUT THE AUTHOR

(Photo by Russell Jeffcoat)

JERRED METZ GREW UP in New Jersey. He studied and taught at the University of Rhode Island and the University of Minnesota. He taught at Webster College and the University of Pittsburgh. For fifteen years he was poetry editor of the *Webster Review*. He was a founder of Singing Bone Press. In addition to writing and teaching, Metz served as the deputy director of the Department of Human Services, St. Louis, Missouri; program director for the Cardinal Ritter Institute, St. Louis; and director of the North Winds Institute for Breathing Practices and Breath Studies in Pittsburgh. He now teaches in South Carolina at Webster University and Coker College.

೮ ೮ ೮   Notes on the production of this book   ೮ ೮ ೮

This book was printed simultaneously in two editions.

A *special limited hardcover edition* of only 400 copies was Symth sewn and bound in Blackberry Kidskin Kivar 7, embossed with burnished Dakota Copper foil, and wrapped in a four-color dustjacket.
The special edition contains a High Plains Press limited edition bookplate printed on archival paper, designed from a woodcut by Richard Wagener. Each bookplate is individually signed by the author and hand-numbered.

A *softcover trade edition* was issued simultaneously. It is covered with twelve-point stock, printed in four colors, and coated with a special gloss finish.

The text of all editions is composed in eleven-point Adobe Garamond. Display type is Billhead Nineteen Hundred, Billhead Nineteen Ten, and Euphoria all by LHF.
The book is printed on Glatfelter sixty-pound Nature's Natural, a recycled, acid-free paper, by Thomson Shore, a participant in the Green Press Initiative.

 **green press** I N I T I A T I V E

High Plains Press is committed to preserving ancient forests and natural resources. We elected to print *The last eleven days of Earl Durand* on 50% post consumer recycled paper, processed chlorine free. As a result, for this printing, we have saved:

26 trees (40' tall and 6-8" diameter)
11,092 gallons of water
4,461 kilowatt hours of electricity
1,223 pounds of solid waste
2,402 pounds of greenhouse gases

High Plains Press made this paper choice because our printer, Thomson-Shore, Inc., is a member of Green Press Initiative, a nonprofit program dedicated to supporting authors, publishers, and suppliers in their efforts to reduce their use of fiber obtained from endangered forests.

For more information, visit www.greenpressinitiative.org